HERE'S HELP!

HAWTHORN BOOKS, INC.
W. Clement Stone, Publisher
New York

× +

When You Bought This Book,
You Bought Stock In Yourself!

The best investment you can make is in YOU.

You can make more money or acquire more of whatever you want—by investing in YOU than in any other investment.

When you bought this book, you bought stock in YOURSELF.

Nobody buys stock in anything unless he or she has *confidence* in it. Because, in buying this book, you really bought stock in YOURSELF, you have proved that you have *confidence* in YOURSELF.

Now that you have bought stock in YOUR-SELF and proved that you have *confidence* in YOUR-SELF, you have taken the first step in getting *whatever you want in life*.

This book now will tell you *how* to do it.

× +

YOURSELF STOCK CERTIFICATE

This certifies that you own

1,000,000 shares

of

STOCK IN YOURSELF

This is your certificate of confidence in your-self and your agreement to begin at once and to continue constantly to use positive success metods to get whatever you want as a worthy life goal.

HERE'S HELP!

Contents

93 chapters of personal help:

Chapter	Title	Page

Chapter 1

Here's HELP! . . .

This Book Is A Treasure Chest Filled With PROVEN SUCCESS METHODS

Many years ago, I began my business career as an office boy, earning $45 a month.

I knew, even then, that the ONLY SURE WAY TO SUCCEED was:

(1) *Learn* (*or have available*) *every* PROVEN SUCCESS METHOD . . .

(2) *Constantly use as many* PROVEN SUCCESS METHODS *as possible*.

That was something even a $45-a-month office boy could *begin* to do.

So I did.

I began learning (and writing down for study and reference) *every* PROVEN SUCCESS METHOD which I could find.

I devoted 40 years to researching every source.

As the result of my 40 years of research to find and record every PROVEN SUCCESS METHOD, *I now own 3 private libraries and 15 personal files* of PROVEN SUCCESS METHODS.

I shall not take the space here to describe the details of my search for every PROVEN SUCCESS METHOD, nor is a detailed description necessary—because *you* do not need to devote 40 years to this research.

You NOW have the results in your hands!

At least you have as many of the PROVEN SUCCESS METHODS as I could put into one book.

I have written other books to be a matched set with this book—as a compact PROVEN SUCCESS METHODS LIBRARY. These are now available.

Each of my other books contains more and, of course, *different* PROVEN SUCCESS METHODS.

Additional books will be written and published until *every* PROVEN SUCCESS METHOD, *which I found and recorded in 40 years of research,* will be available to every ambitious person—in fulfillment of *my own life-goal to help millions of worthy people succeed.*

Now, let's review the ONLY SURE WAY TO SUCCEED to see how its works in real life:

(1) *Learn (or have available) every* PROVEN SUCCESS METHOD . . .

(2) *Constantly use as many* PROVEN SUCCESS METHODS *as possible* . . .

This I did.

And this is the result to date:

Beginning as a $45-a-month office boy, I even-

2

tually became president of 8 corporations and success counselor to 102 companies.

I am the author of major books (like this one) which make available to all ambitious people, the PROVEN SUCCESS METHODS which I researched and recorded over a period of 40 years, including the years after my early retirement.

To control the publishing and distribution of this vast treasure of PROVEN SUCCESS METHODS, I established my own publishing company.

At the age of fifty, I retired from all other businesses to devote my full time to helping others succeed. I continued—and still continue—researching PROVEN SUCCESS METHODS.

I am the author of articles in national magazines and in nationally syndicated newspaper features on how to succeed. I contribute to the contents of university text books.

Thus, I am able to reach millions of readers and fulfill my life-goal of *helping millions of ambitious people succeed*—and I have become known as *America's Success Counselor*.

Mrs. Kopmeyer and I have established the *M. R. Kopmeyer Foundation*, a perpetual trust fund through which our estates can be used for already specified charitable purposes—so that our work to help others will continue beyond our own lifetimes.

This I have accomplished simply by using the ONLY SURE WAY TO SUCCEED:

(1) *Learn* (*or have available*) *every* PROVEN SUCCESS METHOD . . .

(2) *Constantly use as many* PROVEN SUC-CESS METHODS *as possible.*

YOU can accomplish much more than I have, because:

(a) You do not have to start as a $45-a-month office boy, as I did, and . . .

(b) You do not have to devote 40 years to research, as I did, to find and record every PROVEN SUCCESS METHOD, because I am making them available to you in this and my other books . . . NOW!

You NOW have in *this* book and available in my other books—*all* of the PROVEN SUCCESS METHODS *you ever will need* to enable you to:

(1) Attain your *life-goal,* WHATEVER it is!

(2) *Become* the person you WANT to be!

(3) *Get WHATEVER you want!*

(4) *Succeed* with PEOPLE-PROBLEMS!

(5) *Manage* and, if it is necessary, *control* PROBLEM-PEOPLE!

(6) *Manage* and *control* YOURSELF so that you can *successfully master ANY personal problems!*

(7) Achieve and maintain INNER PEACE so that you will be *at peace with yourself and with your fellow men!*

Here's HELP! . . .

This book is power-packed with PROVEN SUCCESS METHODS to enable you to achieve *any or all* of the above goals—and *any other worthy life-goal!*

You now have the methods in your hands. Your success will depend upon how *constantly* you USE them. Start using these success methods now!

Chapter 2

Here's HELP! . . .

Why PROVEN SUCCESS METHODS Will Always Succeed For You

Let's get this settled *first*—at the beginning of this book.

You have a right to ask, "Will PROVEN SUCCESS METHODS *always* succeed?"

The answer is: *"Yes!"*

You have a right to ask if PROVEN SUCCESS METHODS *specifically* will succeed for *you.*

Again the answer is: "Yes!" To which must be added the requirement that you *really USE them.* Not just sometimes. Not if you happen to think about them. But *constantly! Persistently! Consistently! Always!*

Let's lay it right on the line:

You have to make a career of being successful!

5

Of course, *you* choose *what* you want to succeed in achieving.

The terrific advantage of using PROVEN SUCCESS METHODS is that you can choose *whatever* you want to accomplish in life—and *know* you will be successful in accomplishing it!

Your present does not limit your future!

You can start in poverty and become a millionaire!

You can change from a life of crime to become a great evangelist!

You can start from being an uneducated dropout and reach the heights of educational attainment and intellectual honors!

You can go from *wherever* you are now to *wherever* you want to go!

There are two requirements:

(1) As the great Harvard psychologist, William James, taught: "If you only CARE ENOUGH for the result, *you will attain it.* If you wish to be rich, you will be rich; if you wish to be learned, you will be learned; if you wish to be good, you will be good. *Only you must really wish these things.*"

That is the first principle of *succeeding* in becoming *whatever* you want to be . . . in getting *whatever* you want in life . . . in attaining your life-goal. You must *really* CARE ENOUGH!

(2) The second requirement of *certain* success is based on the first.

You must CARE ENOUGH *to do what?*

You must CARE ENOUGH—you must *really*

want to succeed so very much that you will *constantly* . . . *persistently* . . . *consistently* . . . *use* PROVEN SUCCESS METHODS.

So now we come to the absolute reason *why* PROVEN SUCCESS METHODS *always succeed*—and therefore *specifically* will succeed for YOU.

Let us begin with the most basic of fundamental principles:

Everything exists, operates, produces results in conformance to unchanging *Universal Laws*.

These are the laws which operate the entire universe—*Infinite Principles*—which control the unlimited universe in endless space for eternity.

These unchanging *Universal Laws* control *everything* from the countless galaxies in outer space to the everyday events of your life.

Universal Laws (or *Infinite Principles,* if you prefer to call them that) apply to *everything*—including, of course, *everything that affects your life.*

For example:

(a) There are *Universal PHYSICAL Laws,* such as the *Law of Gravity,* the *Law of Cause and Effect,* and countless more, including the *Law of Physical Life,* itself.

(b) There are *Universal MENTAL Laws,* including the *Law of Interrelated Minds* which operates the interconnection between your conscious mind, subconscious mind and the *Infinite Mind* (from which you can *channel unlimited power* as explained in later chapters of this book). They include *Mind Power* which can *materialize thoughts into realities,* as also is explained in this book.

7

(c) There are *Universal EMOTIONAL Laws,* including the *Law of Psychosomatics* which governs the physical illnesses that are caused by such emotions as anxiety, anger, hatred and other illness-producing emotions, as also is explained in later chapters.

(d) There are *Universal SPIRITUAL Laws* which govern man's relation to God, Infinity, Eternity.

That these *Universal Laws* exist, there is no doubt. The vast universe, itself, could not exist, without unchanging *Laws* (or *Principles*) which maintain its eternal existence and its perpetual operation with infinite precision.

Having stated the foregoing, let me hasten to assure the reader that it is not the purpose of this book to presume to explain the incomprehensible mysteries of the Universe—but simply to establish, at the beginning, that:

(1) There *are* unchanging *Universal Laws.*

(2) PROVEN SUCCESS METHODS based on unchanging *Universal Laws* will produce *predictable, absolutely certain results in your* life.

The PROVEN SUCCESS METHODS in this book are simply *Universal Laws* applied in "method" form to human problems and goals—for practical, easy, everyday use by everyone.

There is not *anything* mysterious, complicated or difficult about PROVEN SUCCESS METHODS.

The PROVEN SUCCESS METHODS in this book are simple, clear, concise, easy-to-read, easy to understand—and, most important of all, *easy-to-use* NOW to enable *you* to achieve the successful results and goals listed in the preceding chapter.

So that there can be no doubt about the exact purpose of this book, I want to repeat here *what* the PROVEN SUCCESS METHODS in this book *will enable YOU to do:*

(1) Attain your *life-goal,* WHATEVER it is!

(2) *Become* the person you WANT to be!

(3) *Get WHATEVER you want!*

(4) *Succeed* with PEOPLE-PROBLEMS!

(5) *Manage* and, if it is necessary, *control* PROBLEM-PEOPLE!

(6) *Manage* and *control* YOURSELF so that you can *successfully master ANY personal problems!*

(7) Achieve and maintain INNER PEACE so that you will be *at peace with yourself and with your fellow men!*

The PROVEN SUCCESS METHODS in this book will enable you to do any or all of the foregoing, because these methods—although they are easy to understand and easy to use—are simple, everyday applications in "method" form of the unchanging and absolute *Universal Laws* which control everything, everywhere, eternally. Here is *unlimited* power YOU can use!

How you can use unchanging, all-powerful *Universal Laws,* simplified in PROVEN SUCCESS METHODS, to attain your life-goal—*whatever* your goal —is explained in the next chapters. . .

Chapter 3

Here's HELP! . . .

YOU Can Attain Your Life-Goal

Yes! YOU can attain your life-goal!

YOU can attain your life-goal no matter what your *present* circumstances are.

If you have a high life-goal and a low beginning—that's good.

That's *good?* Why?

Because people who must *overcome difficulties* have more need and more motivation to *try harder*.

Psychologists call this "over-compensation", which simply means "extra-trying" or *trying harder* in order to overcome difficulties.

J. Paul Getty, who is a billionaire (equal to 1,000 millionaires), says that the *secret of success* is just two words: TRY HARDER!

Anyone, anywhere, can *try harder*.

The greater your difficulties, the *harder you*

need to try to overcome them. And, *the harder you try, the more you succeed!*

Your rate (speed) of succeeding will be greater. And you will attain your goal in life much faster *if your present situation or the magnitude of your goal forces you or motivates you to TRY HARDER.*

It usually works out in real life that *people with the most difficulties to overcome also have the greatest opportunities*—because they have the *greatest need* and the *most incentive* to *try harder.*

They have the greatest opportunity to *fail* if they DO NOT *try harder*—and the greatest opportunity to *succeed* if they DO *try harder.*

They can develop more *success momentum*—a faster *rate* of succeeding—than people with less difficulties to overcome who do not think they need to try as hard.

Over the years, people who *need to try harder* and therefore have *more success momentum*, always pass those who thought they did not need to try as hard and therefore developed *less success momentum.*

But anyone—*everyone!*—can attain his or her goal in life. By TRYING HARDER!

Of course, there is more—*much more*—and *it is taught in other chapter-lessons* of this book. But the *essential* and *first* lesson in attaining your life-goal is: TRY HARDER!

Once you are motivated to TRY HARDER—*using the proven success methods which this book will teach you*—then you are *certain* to achieve ANY goal you can conceive and in which you believe.

However, it is desirable for everyone to know

at the beginning that people who have the most difficulties to overcome also have the greatest opportunities.

Because they have the greatest *need to try harder*, those who do try harder often "over-compensate" (*try extra hard*) and develop *terrific success momentum* directly to their life-goals, passing those with better starts.

So the real challenge is to those who have fewer difficulties—because it is they who must generate *SELF-motivation* or they will find themselves stuck in complacency.

Whatever is your own goal in life, you *can* attain it—because of, or in spite of, your *present* circumstances.

The first requirement is *desire*.

If you *want* to attain your goal earnestly enough to *try harder* . . . and *try harder* . . . and *try harder*—using the proven success methods taught in this book—*YOU WILL GENERATE THE MEANS AND THE POWER* to achieve *any goal* which you can conceive and in which you believe!

So let's begin with *How To BECOME What You Want To Be* . . . which is the next chapter. . .

Chapter 4

Here's HELP! . . .

How To BECOME What You Want To Be

There is something in each of us which *requires* fulfillment.

It is an inner urge to become *our best possible self,* to live our life on *our finest level!*

Each of us has an inner drive *toward personal greatness!* Since this is a subconscious drive, it may not surface completely into our daily consciousness. Many people never learn that they even have it!

But our inner drive to greatness is there—below the level of our conscious awareness. Our subconscious, being cybernetic (which means goal seeking), *strives to fulfill it.*

Yet many people do not *act* to improve themselves so that they reach the personal greatness which *could* be theirs.

They settle for mediocrity—or worse. This

causes an inner conflict between *what they are* and *the greatness which their inner drive wants to produce in their lives!*

So frustration comes to live with them.

As any psychiatrist will tell you, when you ignore or deny a subconscious urge, you incur a nagging feeling of frustration. You have a constant, disturbing feeling that something is *wrong* in your life (*and it is!*). You feel that you should *do* something about it (*and you should!*).

What must you do?

Here's HELP! . . .

In a recent psychological research project, the purpose was to determine if I Q could be greatly increased. (The study proved that it could—which should be a challenge to all those who have been using the excuse that they were not "*born* smart".)

What is more important, the distinguished psychological researcher also concluded: "People have a *self-image* and *BECOME what they envision themselves* to be."

"*Envision*" means to "*mentally picture*".

So, how do you BECOME what you want to be?

By *frequently* (as constantly as possible) *mentally picturing yourself as being what you want to BE-COME*.

To be successful, you *must* mentally picture yourself as being successful. You cannot succeed if you mentally picture yourself as a failure—as a failure now or in the future.

This is a universal law: the *Law of Consistency*.

You cannot think (mentally picture) one thing and *be*—or *do*—another.

You cannot *"think poor"* and become rich.

You cannot think *"love"* and feel hate.

So . . . the first requirement of fulfilling your inner drive (which you may not consciously know you have) is to *mentally picture* yourself as actually *being* what you want to BECOME.

And when you mentally picture the kind of person you *want* to become: THINK BIG!

Your imagination will place *no limit* on your mental picture.

Life will place *no limit* on its realization.

The universal *Law of Consistency* requires that you will BECOME *whatever* you *mentally picture*. You cannot—*you will not*—become anything else, nothing more, nothing less.

So . . . THINK BIG! Do not settle for mediocrity. Do not accept (by mentally picturing) less than the *greatest goal you want to achieve!*

You can become *whatever* you want to be, because your THOUGHTS (mental pictures) *control your life and determine your future* . . . which is the lesson of the next chapter . . .

Chapter 5

Here's HELP! . . .

Your THOUGHTS (Mental Pictures) Control Your Life; Determine Your Future

Your THOUGHTS—which you inwardly "see" as *mental pictures*—control your life and determine your future. They form the *mental blueprint* which directs how your life will be built. It cannot be otherwise.

This is the teaching throughout history.

The Bible says so. The Bible teaches, "As a man *thinketh,* so *is* he."

You *think* with *mental pictures.* Every *thought* is a *mental picture* projected into your subconscious.

Every *mental picture* is your instruction to your subconscious to guide your life in the direction of your mental picture until *your mental picture becomes a reality.*

So the Bible teaches, "As a man *thinketh* (with *mental pictures*), so *is* he."

16

It is the teaching of *all* religions that we *become* what we *think* (*mentally picture*).

Buddha taught, '*All* (yes, *all*) that we *are* is the result of what we have *thought* (*mentally pictured*)."

All of the great thinkers, scholars, philosophers and wise men throughout history have affirmed that every person *becomes* what he or she *thinks* (*mentally pictures*).

Wrote, the great emperor and philosopher of ancient Rome, Marcus Aurelius: "Our *life* is what our *thoughts make it.*" And so it is. Our thoughts are *mental pictures* projected into the subconscious which *guides us to*—or *attracts to us*—our *self-image*.

The latest discoveries of modern psychology prove this fact over and over again: "People have a *self-image* and *become what they envision themselves to be.*"

"*Envision*" means to "*mentally picture*". You *become* what you *envision* (*mentally picture*) *yourself to be*.

The famous psychologist, William James of Harvard, stated it this way: "*Belief* (*an intense mental picture*) *creates the actual fact.*" He said, "*Actual fact.*"

Emerson, one of the wisest Americans, stated categorically: "*Thoughts* (*mental pictures*) *rule the world.*" Powerful things—those *mental pictures* of yours!

And the famous clergyman, William Ellery Channing, wrote, "What a man *does outwardly* is but the *expression* and *completion* of his *inward thought* (*mental pictures*)." You act, do, achieve or fail as the *outward expression* of your *inner mental pictures*.

Your *mental pictures* are *completed* into reality by being *converted into power* by your subconscious. As

Emerson stated it: "There is no *thought* (*mental picture*) in any mind, but it quickly tends to *convert itself* into a *power*." It is that *mental-picture-power* which enables you to guide your life confidently to your goal.

Jonathan Edwards stated that our *mental pictures constantly govern* each of us. To quote him exactly: "The ideas and images in men's minds (*mental pictures*) *are the invisible powers that constantly govern them*." This means that, through your mental pictures, you govern (control) your life.

So as the world-famous preacher-psychologist-writer, Dr. Norman Vincent Peale, says, "Think success, visualize (*mentally picture*) success, and you will set in motion the power force of the realizable wish. When the *mental picture* or attitude is strongly enough held, it actually seems to *control conditions and circumstances*."

Thousands of years of wisdom, experience, observation and research have proven, beyond any doubt, that YOU WILL BECOME WHAT YOU MENTALLY PICTURE.

What was revealed to the ancient wise men . . . what was learned during the thousands of years of study, experience and observation . . . and what has been proven again and again by modern science, psychology and psychiatry—is that YOUR FUTURE WILL BE WHAT YOU MENTALLY PICTURE IT WILL BE.

Chapter 6

Here's HELP! . . .

You "Plant" Mental Pictures And You Reap Whatever You Plant

Heed the wise proverb: *"You can harvest ONLY what you plant."* It is the universal *Law of Consistency*.

If you plant corn, it would not be *consistent* for you to harvest beans. It only would be *consistent* for corn to grow from seed-corn. So planting corn can *only* produce corn.

The universal *Law of Consistency* applies to *everything* in life.

Some examples:

If you "plant" mental pictures of your being a failure, you will "harvest" a crop of failures. You could not possibly succeed because that would be *inconsistent* with your mental pictures of your being a failure. You only could—and *would*—fail.

If you "plant" mental pictures of your being

19

and *remaining* poor, you will get *only* what you plant: *poverty*. You cannot constantly "plant" thoughts (mental) pictures) of *poverty* in your goal-producing subconscious, and expect a harvest of riches to grow from your constant mental pictures of *poverty*.

The *Law of Consistency* will not permit mental pictures of poverty to produce wealth any more that it will permit seed-corn to grow up to be beans.

So . . . mental pictures of poverty can ONLY produce poverty in your life.

If you think poor, you will be poor.

If you think success, you will be successful.

If you think rich, you will be rich.

If you think goodwill, you will attract goodwill in return.

If you think friendship, you will attract friends.

If you think love, you will be loved.

It is so. It is in accordance with the universal *Law of Consistency*. It cannot be otherwise.

It is in accordance with the Bible: "As a man THINKETH, so IS he."

It is in accordance with all religions, all philosophy, all psychology, all wisdom, all science, all history, all research . . .

YOU WILL BECOME WHAT YOU MOST FREQUENTLY THINK (MENTALLY PICTURE) YOU WILL BE.

Chapter 7

Here's HELP! . . .

Your Thoughts Are MENTAL PICTURES! Here's How They Guide Your Life!

When you think, you visualize a *mental picture* of what you think.

This is not just an academic lesson in elementary psychology. It is the beginning of the revelation of a PROVEN SUCCESS METHOD which will enable *you to control your life and determine your future!*

So, proceed with great expectations—because *your great expectations will become realities!*

When you think of a house, you do not think the word-letters: H-O-U-S-E. You visualize (mentally picture) a house. You *mentally picture* an actual house . . . a house you own . . . or a house you would like to own . . . or an imaginary "dream house" . . . or some house, which for some reason, comes to mind as a *mental picture.*

Even in the unlikely possibility that you would think only of the spelling H-O-U-S-E, you would *mentally picture* the alphabetical letters.

Or, as another example: you *mentally picture* a *hate-situation* (past, present, real or imagined). You visualize *yourself* experiencing the emotion of hate and *"acting out" in your imagination* (mentally picturing) what you consciously or subconsciously would *like* to do because of hate.

We could list other examples endlessly. But it will be more effective for you to visualize your own examples and examine the *mental picture* which each *projects on the "picture screen" of your mind.*

As you do this, realize that the *"picture-screen" of your mind is your subconscious.*

Your subconscious "remembers"—and under circumstances which we shall describe later in this book—can use its cybernetic (goal-seeking) powers *to guide you to,* or *attract to you,* whatever you repeatedly and intensely project in *mental pictures* on its "picture screen."

This mental "picture screen" of your subconscious is your life-guidance system which can and will *materialize your mental pictures into reality.*

So when the Bible declares, "As a man *thinketh* (mentally pictures), so *is* he" . . . the Bible is affirming a spiritual fact, a psychological fact, a physical fact.

It is true, beyond any possibility of doubt, that YOU BECOME WHAT YOU THINK . . . which means that *you become what you mentally picture, because your thoughts ARE mental pictures.*

This book will teach you HOW to use *deliber-*

ately controlled mental pictures: (1) to attain your life-goal, (2) to become what you want to be, (3) to get whatever you want.

Of course, you will have to do more than project mental pictures into your life-guiding subconscious. This book will teach you the other PROVEN SUCCESS METHODS to make your mental pictures realities.

But you must *start*—and *continue*—to mentally picture what you want, otherwise whatever else you do will have no direction.

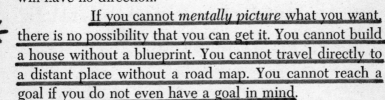

If you cannot *mentally picture* what you want, there is no possibility that you can get it. You cannot build a house without a blueprint. You cannot travel directly to a distant place without a road map. You cannot reach a goal if you do not even have a goal in mind.

If you cannot, will not, or do not *first* concentrate your thoughts on your life-goal, on what you want to be, on what you want in life—you will wander aimlessly through life . . . *lost on your way to nowhere!*

That is why the first part of this book is about the first thing you must do:

YOU MUST GUIDE YOUR LIFE WITH MENTAL PICTURES!

In the next chapter, *you become the SUPER-STAR of your own mental movie* . . .

Chapter 8

Here's HELP! . . .

Your Mind Is A MENTAL MOVIE And YOU Are The SUPERSTAR!

As you know, your thoughts lead into each other.

One thought suggests a related thought which suggests a thought related to it . . . and so on . . . and on . . . one thought leading to another.

As explained in preceding chapters, *your thoughts are mental pictures.*

Mental pictures in a continuous sequence are *mental movies.*

These *mental movies*—projected intensely and repeatedly upon the mental "picture screen" of your subconscious—*are materialized into reality* in your life.

And so, as Marcus Aurelius, one of the wisest men in all history, stated many centuries ago: *"Our life is what our thoughts (mental pictures) make it."*

Or as modern psychologists affirm, "People

have a *self-image* and *become what they envision* (*mentally picture*) *themselves to be.*"

History and modern science agree that this is so. It is the universal *Law of Consistency*.

It is important for you to realize that you do not envision *just one mental picture*—but a continuous sequence of mental pictures—*a mental movie.*

So you are not sitting for a self-portrait of *one mental picture*—but *you* are the SUPERSTAR of *your own mental movie* which will *materialize as your future!*

What *kind* of SUPERSTAR will *you* be in your own *mental movie?*

Will you project a *mental movie* of YOU, SUPERSTAR as a failure? . . . a drop-out? . . . a coward? . . . a weakling?

Or, will you project a *mental movie* of YOU, SUPERSTAR as a success? . . . a master of problems and problem-people . . . master of yourself . . . a PROVEN SUCCESS METHOD person . . . who can *get what you want* . . . and *be what you want to be* . . . and *attain your goal in life!*

What kind of SUPERSTAR will *you* be?

The choice is yours because *you control the mental movie* which you project on the "picture screen" of your subconscious.

And you choose the *kind* of SUPERSTAR you will be in your own mental movie which will become your life. And so you determine your own future.

Remember that the universal *Law of Consistency* will cause you to be *in real life* exactly the kind of person you picture yourself to be *in your mind.*

If your dominant thoughts are of *failure,* you will constantly re-play in your mind a mental movie of *failure.* And YOU, SUPERSTAR, will "act out" in your mental movie your shabby performance as a *failure.*

Then, you can *ONLY be a failure* in a real life of *failure*—because your real life *must be consistent* with what you mentally picture it to be. It cannot be otherwise.

If YOU, SUPERSTAR, "act out" the role of *failure* in your thoughts, in your mental movie, *you can ONLY be a failure*—because the *Law of Consistency* requires that you can ONLY *become* what is *consistent* with how you "*see*" yourself.

BUT . . .

If your dominant thoughts are of your being or becoming *successful,* you will constantly re-play in your mind a mental movie of *your being successful!* And YOU, SUPERSTAR, will "act out" in your mental movie your brilliant performance as a *big success!*

Then you can *ONLY be a success* in a real life of *success!*

Because your real life *must be consistent* with what you mentally picture it to be. It cannot be otherwise.

If YOU, SUPERSTAR, "act out" the role of *success* in your thoughts, in your mental movie, *you can ONLY be a success*—because the *Law of Consistency* requires that you can ONLY *become* what is *consistent* with how you "*see*" yourself.

The mental pictures which you "plant" in your subconscious life-guidance system will grow into a real-life harvest of *whatever* you plant. *Exactly that!*

Just as you cannot plant corn and expect to

harvest beans, you cannot "plant" mental pictures of failure and expect to harvest success in real life.

If you think poor, you will be poor.

If you think rich, you will be rich.

If you think success, you will be successful.

If you think goodwill, you will attract goodwill.

If you think friendship, you will attract friends.

If you think love, you will be loved.

It is so. It is in accordance with the *Law of Consistency*. It cannot be otherwise.

"As a man THINKETH, so IS he."

Chapter 9

Here's HELP! . . .

How The "Three Minds" MATERIALIZE Your MENTAL PICTURES Into Reality

There are three "stages" or "levels" of Mind Power. These three levels of Mind Power are *described sparately* in this chapter, however, *they are not separate but actually blend into each other.* They are inter-related parts of *one Universal Mind.*

These three levels of Mind Power are:

(1) Your *conscious mind.* This is your brain. It can be exposed by brain surgery and examined directly, or it can be studied indirectly through psychological tests. It is the part of your mind with which you *consciosuly think.*

Your *conscious mind* can deliberately project your *mental pictures* upon the "picture screen" of your subconscious.

You can consciously visualize your mental pic-

tures and you can consciously control your mental pictures.

(2) Your *subconscious mind.* This is the part of your mind which operates regardless of your conscious control, *but which can be directed by your conscious mind, using mental pictures visualized by conscious thought.*

Your *subconscious mind* performs so many functions we cannot describe them all, but here are a few.

Your *subconscious* is in complete control of your life—which includes directing your complex bodily functions: heart-beat, breathing, digestion, and *everything which your living requires.*

If you had to depend upon your *conscious* mind to think: "Now I instruct my heart to beat . . . now I instruct my lungs to breathe . . . now I instruct my stomach to digest food, etc., etc., etc. . . ." you could not manage, even for a minute, the *trillions* of sensorium nerve impulses required to maintain your life. You would be dead in a minute.

So, Nature, with an intelligence which we cannot even begin to comprehend, has provided the *subconscious.* It is the *Something* which connects limited man with unlimited *Infinity* and therefore is a channel to *Infinite Intelligence* and *Infinite Power* to the extent that man can humanly understand and use it.

Your *subconscious* is your channel to *all* of the means and power you *ever* will need for *anything!*

Your *subconscious* is a memory storehouse which retains *every* thought and image you *ever* have *mentally pictured*—even if your *conscious mind* has completely forgotten. This is proved by the capability of psychoanalysis to probe your forgotten past all of the way back through your early childhood.

Your *mental pictures,* past and present, are arranged through your *subconscious,* by some incomprehensible method, *to become the "building blocks" of your life,* each in its own size and importance according to the *intensity* of each *mental picture* when it was projected into your *subconscious.*

The wisdom of recorded religion and philosophy throughout history has proclaimed what modern psychologists now affirm, based on the latest psychological research: "People have a *self-image* and BECOME what they *envision (mentally picture)* themselves to be." In psychology, *"envision"* means *"mentally picture."* So psychologists state that you BECOME what you *mentally picture.* It is the universal *Law of Consistency.*

What you are now is the result of the *kind* and the *intensity* of *mental pictures* which you—deliberately or carelessly—projected into your *subconscious* throughout your life to this time.

For better or for worse!

Your subconscious does not reason; it accepts, without judgment, the mental pictures which you furnish it with which to build your life.

If you do not like what *you are now*—remember that it was *your mental pictures* in the past which produced you as *you are now,* and made your life what *it now is!* You made your present; you can make your future.

You can improve yourself and your life—*starting right now*—by improving the *kind* and the *intensity* of your *mental pictures.*

Future chapter-lessons will teach you HOW to do it—deliberately, surely, easily.

But let us conclude this chapter by naming the third and highest level of Mind. It cannot be described because it is beyond human description . . . beyond human comprehension . . . because it is . . .

(3) *The Infinite Mind.* We cannot even begin to comprehend *Infinity* because it is . . . space without limit . . . time eternal, without beginning or end . . . *all* power . . . *all* knowledge . . . *everything* . . . *everywhere* . . . *always.*

Infinity is all-inclusive.

And that includes each of us—and the means of fulfilling our deepest desires to whatever extent we can conceive and believe.

To briefly review:

There are three levels of Mind Power—or the *Three Minds*—through which your *mental pictures* are materialized to become your life:

(1) Your *conscious mind*

(2) Your *subconscious mind*

(3) *The Infinite Mind*

It will help you understand the individual and related functions of the *Three Minds* if you think of them this way:

(1) Your *conscious mind* provides the *"management"* which decides what you want to acquire and what you want to become. These are decisions which you *deliberately* and *consciously* make.

Your *conscious mind* (the "management" part of your mind) transmits its instructions through *mental pictures* to . . .

(2) Your *subconscious mind,* which is your

"life manufacturing factory". Your *subconscious mind* accepts, without question, your *mental pictures* (whatever they are) *as absolute instructions to produce them as your life* and it procedes to do so in the same miraculous manner that it operates your heart-beat, your breathing, and all of your life functions.

Your *subconscious mind* has the unlimited means and power to guide you to, or attract to you, whatever you intensely and constantly project as *mental pictures of your life-goal.* In fact, it cannot do otherwise.

This is in accordance with the universal *Law of Consistency* which requires that your *mind-commands* (mental pictures) which you "plant as seeds" in your subconscious *produce exactly what you plant*—so that what you harvest is *consistent* with what you plant.

It is *Universal Law,* part of the infallible . . .

(3) *Infinite Mind,* which is the *total intelligence of the universe*—the all-prevading intelligence which is in every cell, in every miniscule unit of matter, energy— yes, and spirit. Call it *soul.* Call it *God.* Name it what you will; it is *Infinite,* and *you communicate with it through your subconscious with mental pictures.*

You may think of this communicating with the *Infinite*—as prayer.

And since this form of communication is through *mental pictures,* you may remember the ancient proverb: "One *picture* is worth *ten thousand words.*"

So, since mental pictures are the most comprehensive form of mental communication between humans, how much more so are they the highest level of communicating with the *Infinite!*

Chapter 10

Here's HELP! . . .

You Can IMAGINE Your Future Into Reality!

Of all the chapters in this book, *this* may be the most important.

Let's be *sure* you get it. *All of it!*

So let's start with a quick review!

(1) Your mind is a continuous mental movie.

(2) Your mental movie consists of mental pictures on the "picture screen" of your subconscious.

(3) Your mental pictures impress themselves *permanently* into your subconscious.

(4) Your subconscious uses your mental pictures cybernetically—which means *your mental pictures become your life-guidance system.*

(5) Your mental pictures, therefore, *determine your future* because they *guide* you to, and *attract* to you, the opportunities, personal contacts, financial and other means you need to reach your goal in life.

(6) *So, your mental pictures actually BE-COME YOUR FUTURE to which they guide you and make possible for you to attain.*

End of review. I suggest you re-read it—preferably *memorize* it.

What you *physically see* is one of three ways in which mental pictures are formed and impressed into your subconscious where they *become part of your life-guidance system to determine your future.*

Here are some examples:

Because the rich *mentally picture* what they *physically see: "The rich get richer."* They constantly *see* the *wealth* which surrounds them. So their mental pictures are of *wealth.* They *"think rich".* So . . . *the rich get richer.*

And, because the poor *mentally picture* what they *physically see: "The poor get poorer."* They constantly *see* the *poverty* which surrounds them. So their mental pictures are of *poverty.* They *"think poor".* So . . . *"the poor get poorer".*

UNLESS . . .

The poor change their mental pictures and impress mental pictures of SUCCESS into their subconscious, because . . .

Mental pictures of SUCCESS will guide the poor out of poverty and to success, wealth, leadership—*whatever they want!*

Why is this so?

It is a Universal Law . . . the Law of Consistency.

"Planting" mental pictures into the subconscious is like planting seeds. *You harvest ONLY what you plant*. So, if you plant corn, ONLY corn will grow. The *Law of Consistency* requires that what you plant must— *to be consistent*—produce a harvest of ONLY what you plant.

And "planting" mental pictures into your subconscious will produce a harvest in your life of ONLY what you mentally picture. It cannot be otherwise, because it must be *consistent*.

So it does no good (except for temporary emotional release) to organize the poor into groups and lead them in the now-familiar chant: "I am POOR . . . but I am somebody!"

At the very best, that would cause them to mentally picture that they are "somebody who is POOR". And, that's exactly what they are already—and want to change!

It would be better if the poor were taught the success methods of this book—*and motivated to USE them!*

Certainly, what people *physically see* in their surroundings becomes mental pictures—but these VISUALLY produced mental pictures *need not be dominant, and can be subjugated by the much more powerful mental pictures deliberately produced by the IMAGINATION.*

You can *deliberately* produce *much more powerful, dominant, vivid, controlled mental pictures* in your IMAGINATION.

Note that you can do this *deliberately*.

You can visualize mental pictures by *deliberately* IMAGINING them.

Because you can produce mental pictures *deliberately*—simply by IMAGINING them—*you can con-*

trol your mental pictures. You can IMAGINE *whatever* mental pictures you *choose* to IMAGINE.

Thus *you* are in full and complete *control* of the *exact content* and *intensity* of the mental pictures you hold in your IMAGINATION and impress *permanently* into your subconscious—*which will determine your future.*

*IMAGINE mental pictures of *wealth—repeatedly, constantly, intensely—and you will become rich!*

*IMAGINE mental pictures of *success—repeatedly, constantly, intensely—and you will be successful!*

*IMAGINE mental pictures of *popularity—repeatedly, constantly, intensely—and you will be popular!*

*IMAGINE mental pictures of *leadership—repeatedly, constantly, intensely—and you will become a leader!*

*IMPORTANT

*This does not mean that all, or even any, of these good, desirable things will suddenly appear in your life by magic. Or by any sort of hocus-pocus. So do not sit idly holding a basket—waiting for these goodies to fall from the sky.

What the foregoing statements mean—and *what this book specifically teaches*—is that your mind is a continuous mental movie consisting of a constant flow of mental pictures which become a part of your subconscious *life-guidance* system.

Your subconscious uses your mental pictures (good or bad) to cybernetically *direct your life* (for better or worse) so that whatever you picture *becomes real.*

In success-training this is known as *"motivational guidance".*

In psychology this is known as *"attitude pre-conditioning"*.

In behavioral therapy this is known as *"pre-determining behavior"*.

So putting it all together in technical terminology, what your mental pictures do in your subconscious is to provide motivational guidance through pre-conditioning your attitude so that you will act in a predetermined manner to achieve the objective which you—repeatedly, constantly, intensely—mentally picture.

Or, to state it simply, *your mental pictures guide you to the reality of WHATEVER you—repeatedly constantly, intensely—mentally picture.*

Note that your mental pictures *guide* you. You must *respond* to their *guidance*. You cannot be *guided* if you do *not respond*. You must *respond* by DOING—not by *waiting* for a miracle.

You were *guided* by your subconscious to purchase this book. But simply *owning* this book will not bring you success.

Nor will just *reading* this book bring you success. You must DO what the book teaches. Not just *read* about it—but DO it!

The title of this book is HERE'S HELP! This book provides the HELP. You must USE its help to succeed.

This book will *teach* you; it will *enable* you. But *you* must DO what it *teaches* and *enables* you to DO.

Learning PROVEN SUCCESS METHODS —as necessary as that is—does not, *in itself*, solve your problems and enable you to get whatever you want. You must USE what you learn. You must DO what this book *enables* you to DO.

There is a *Law of Life* which states: "*DO* the thing—and you will *have* the power."

USE the PROVEN SUCCESS METHODS in this book and my other books—you will RECEIVE the power.

The power to achieve is generated by DOING; you generate *no* power by NOT DOING. As you DO—you will RECEIVE.

So, DO this . . . USE your imagination to *keep* your mind *filled* with *controlled* mental pictures of *whatever you want.*

Your *controlled* mental pictures of whatever you want . . . *success* . . . *wealth* . . . *popularity* . . . *leadership* . . . *whatever you want* . . . will become a permanent part of your *life-guidance* system which will *guide* you directly to your life-goal—if you will just DO what this book teaches.

The teaching of this chapter is that you must USE your IMAGINATION to keep your mind filled with controlled mental pictures of whatever you want.

You must DO this. Not just *read* about it— DO it!

Because if you DO NOT *keep your mind filled with controlled mental pictures of whatever you want—* your *subconscious* will fill your mind with *uncontrolled* and unwanted thoughts of worry, fear, anxiety, discouragement and disturbing uncertainties.

Most people are unhappy because they *"leave their minds open"* for negative thoughts.

Unless you keep your mind *filled* with your *deliberately controlled* mental pictures of what you want— your subconscious will fill it with disturbing mental pictures of what you do *not* want.

Once they get started, *uncontrolled and disturbing mental pictures* may so persistently and completely dominate your mind that you have to literally *"turn them off"*.

The next chapter will teach you how to *"turn off"* disturbing thoughts . . .

Chapter 11

Here's HELP! . . .

How To "Turn Off" Disturbing Thoughts And Unwanted Mental Pictures . . . Instantly

In preceding chapter-lessons, you learned to use *deliberately controlled mental pictures;* to intensely project them on the "picture screen" of your subconscious so that your mental pictures are your life-guidance.

Thus your mental pictures actually guide you into the reality of your future.

It is the recorded conclusion of the entire history of thought: Every person *becomes* what he or she *repeatedly, intensely thinks* (*mentally pictures*).

You *become* WHATEVER you *repeatedly, intensely mentally picture* you will be—*for better or for worse*—depending on the *kind* of *mental picture* you repeatedly, intensely project into your subconscious.

For better or worse.

40

That is the reason for this chapter-lesson.

You learned from preceding chapters that you can *deliberately control* your *mental pictures* if you constantly persist in doing so.

BUT . . . if you do NOT *deliberately control* the mental movie which is the picture sequence of your thought-flow, then *uncontrolled thoughts* (*uncontrolled mental pictures*) will find all mental-spaces *not filled by controlled thoughts.*

These *uncontrolled mental pictures* may be pleasant day dreams, but usually they are mental picture situations of worries, anxieties, fears, resentments, hatreds, or guilt complexes which have been *suppressed* in your subconscious, and which your subconscious takes the first opportunity to release (feed back) into your conscious thought.

This repeats and reinforces NEGATIVE thoughts to become your life-guidance—with disastrous consequences!

Since whatever is *suppressed* in your subconscious is *undesirable* (or it would not be *suppressed*), the worst thing you can do to your future is to *repeat* and *reinforce uncontrolled mental pictures* of *subconscious suppressions* of situations of guilt, anxiety, worry, inferiority, resentment, and hatred into the subconscious management of your life and the materialization of your future!

So you desperately need a sure and instant method of "turning off" negative and undesirable mental pictures.

Here's HELP! . . .

Here's how to do it.

41

To *"turn off"* negative and undesirable *mental pictures* instantly:

(1) *Imagine black:* Think of your mind being *filled* with *total darkness*. Black. *No mental pictures* of disturbing situations. *No mental pictures of any kind.* Blackout *all* mental pictures so that your mind is so filled with deep darkness—*black*—that there is not room for *any* mental picture. *Maintain total mental blackout* until your mind is *relaxed* and *quiet*.

Having thus achieved a QUIET MIND, you *then* can calmly, deliberately replace the temporary darkness with bright, intense, *controlled mental pictures of what you want* as described in preceding chapters.

(2) *Imagine opaque gray:* Some people get better results from "thinking gray" instead of "thinking black". They find gray to be soft and relaxing as it fills their minds *to obscure all mental pictures,* thus producing a QUIET MIND—undisturbed by any mental pictures—a mind at perfect peace.

If you prefer to "think gray" instead of "thinking black", the gray must be *opaque* so that it will *totally* blot out *all* mental pictures, leaving no shadowy forms to distract your attention. *The sole objective is to obliterate mental pictures completely.* Your mind must be *totally filled* with soft, relaxing gray.

(3) *Imagine heavy fog:* Simply "fog-out" all mental pictures. This method has the advantage of sustaining your interest in the "obscuring substance" (fog) and, therefore, away from mental pictures because you begin by filling your mind with whisps of fog, which you mentally turn into thicker, fluffy clouds, and then into

heavy fog which *totally obscures all mental pictures.* Your mind is *completely filled* with dense, impenetrable fog—and *no mental pictures.*

(4) *Imagine any other dark, opaque, non-stimulating color:* The three examples described are preferred because they are neutral and, therefore, non-stimulating. However, if you have a favorite, pleasing color, it may work equally well provided that it is dark and opaque enough to *totally obscure all mental pictures*—leaving no mysterious shadow-pictures to sustain your interest. For example, you can effectively use dark blue or deep purple.

But you must NOT use stimulating colors such as red, yellow, orange—or any bright shade of any color.

The objective is complete mental relaxation while you *entirely obscure all mental pictures* by filling your mind with a neutral, pleasant, opaque color or substance (fog) which *no mental pictures can penetrate.*

Thus, you achieve the *advanced mental-emotional-spiritual level* of QUIET MIND.

As you master thought (mental picture) control so completely that you can produce a QUIET MIND instantly—the benefits to you will be so miraculous that they are indescribable and must be *experienced by you personally!*

One simple benefit of being able to achieve a QUIET MIND instantly—is that *now you can go to sleep in eleven seconds,* even on restless nights—by adding the relaxing methods taught in the next chapter . . .

Chapter 12

Here's HELP! . . .

How To Go To Sleep
In Eleven Seconds!

By using the method taught in the preceding chapter to "turn off" all mental pictures—and combining it with the three easy, natural relaxation progressions taught in this chapter—you will *go to sleep in eleven seconds,* even on restless nights.

I personally use this method to go to sleep in *eleven seconds* every night and whenever I want to take a brief nap.

Anybody can do it, even those tense persons who think they have incurable insomnia when all that's wrong with them is that they do not know *how* to go to sleep. Well, here's *how* to go to sleep:

This easy, instant *four-step* method will enable *anybody* to go to sleep in *eleven seconds.*

It requires *eleven seconds* to complete the following *four* easy, related steps:

(1) *Relax your body:* Use whichever of the widely-recommended body relaxing methods you find most effective . . . go limp . . . or feel heavy . . . or feel light ("float") . . . or whatever body-relaxing method appeals to you. Or just comfortably relax your body in your favorite sleeping position.

(2) *Relax your face:* Be sure to relax your forehead. Particularly relax your jaws so that you do not grit your teeth or let your upper and lower teeth touch.

(3) *More important, relax your eyes:* Lightly close your eyes and be peacefully aware that your eyes have become "blank", totally unemotional, "non-feeling".

(4) *Most important, blank-out all mental pictures:* Your mind must be entirely blank. No mental pictures. Use the methods described in the preceding chapter. *I shall repeat them briefly here because I want to add unusual techniques* which increase their effectiveness when *used to induce sleep.*

(a) *Imagine black:* Think of your mind as being filled with total darkness. Black. All black. The blackness pervades your mind, softly, pleasantly, completely filling it—so if any mental picture tries to visualize, it is enveloped, blurred by the blackness and gently blotted out. Only blackness remains. *And sleep occurs instantly.*

For those who may be uncertain at first, resolute determination may be needed. Impress your mind with your resolve that *you shall continue this method all night*—even if you do not sleep at all. Convince yourself of the truth that, *even if you do not go to sleep at all,* your complete relaxation combined with the blacking out of all mental pictures, *continued all night if necessary,* will be the *equivalent of sound sleep. That* will do it! It cuts off all "escape" and *it is impossible to completely relax and black-out all mental pictures for even eleven seconds without going to sleep.* There simply is no way you can do *that* and stay awake.

Those who have difficulty in imagining their minds *filled* with black, can imagine a large wall covered with soft, black velvet drapery. The soft texture and velvet folds hold your drowsy attention as they conceal all mental pictures for the few seconds until you drift off to sleep.

Or you can add a harmless touch of self-hypnotism. Imagine that across your mind is a large plain black wall. Out of the center of the wall shines a pin-point of very bright light. Keep your attention focused on the bright pin-point of light. *You will fall asleep instantly!*

(b) *Imagine opaque gray:* Some people prefer to "think gray" instead of "thinking black". They find gray to be soft and relaxing. "Thinking gray" will work equally as well as "thinking black" provided that the gray is opaque so that *it will blot out all mental pictures*—which is the sole objective: *no mental pictures.*

You can substitute dark blue or dark purple. The *color* with which you fill your mind must be entirely opaque to obscure *all mental pictures*—leaving no mysterious shadow-pictures to sustain your interest.

Since the sole objective is to achieve *non-stimulation,* you must *not* imagine such stimulating colors as red, yellow, orange—or a *bright* shade of any color.

Remember the purpose: to *"blank-out"* by blocking-out *all mental pictures* by entirely filling your mind with some *imaginary* opaque color or substance which *obscures everything in your mind*—in a totally *non-stimulating* manner.

(c) *Imagine heavy fog:* In this method, you envelop and obscure all mental pictures in a heavy fog which completely fills your mind. "Fogging-out" mental pictures has the advantage of sustaining your concentration on the fog instead of on the mental pictures.

You begin this "fogging-out" of mental pictures by filling your mind with whisps of fog, which you mentally turn into deepening clouds of fluffy fog, and then into heavy fog which *totally obscures all mental pictures.*

Your mind is filled with dense fog through which you mentally can "see" nothing. *No mental pictures.*

INSTANT SLEEP—*in eleven seconds.*

Use the foregoing simple methods and *you will go to sleep in eleven seconds*—even on restless nights.

This will be a life-long benefit to you which directly affects the *one-third of your entire life* which you spend in sleep—or in trying to sleep.

So let's quickly review the simple, easy steps:

(1) *Relax your body*

(2) *Relax your face*

(3) *More important, relax your eyes*

(4) *Most important, blank-out all mental pictures.*

Do these *four* simple, easy things as clearly described in detail in this chapter—*and you will go to sleep in eleven seconds.*

If you do not go to sleep in *eleven seconds*, you are *not properly doing* one or more of the *four* easy steps to instant sleep. It may require a *few more seconds* until you select and perfect the variations which best suit your sleeping comfort, but this method is so easy and so sure that it should not require more than a few nights to reduce your "going-to-sleep" time to *eleven seconds.*

If it requires longer than that, re-read this chapter-lesson until doing the *four* described steps is *automatic.*

Of course, *do not concentrate on the "eleven-second" timing* because then you will be *trying,* and *counting,* and *thinking,* and *become tense—which is the exact opposite of this method*—and will produce the *opposite* of the desired result.

Expect to go to sleep in *eleven seconds*—but *don't count!*

Just relax completely . . . and drowsily go through the four steps . . . and you will be asleep.

It will have taken *eleven seconds*—but you won't know it. *You will be asleep.*

Chapter 13

Here's HELP! . . .

Now . . . INTENSIFY Your Mental Pictures—To Succeed Faster!

In the preceding chapter, you learned how to *"turn off"* your mental pictures so that you could go to sleep in eleven seconds.

In this chapter and in several following chapters you will learn how to *"turn on"* your mental pictures with such *intensity* that they will deeply imprint their *life-guidance instructions* into your subconscious.

It is through your *control* of your mental pictures that you *control* your life and determine your future.

If you leave what you mentally picture to *mere chance,* if you think about *whatever random thoughts aimlessly occupy your mind,* you will find yourself adrift in life at the mercy of events and circumstances *over which you have no control* and concerning which you have no automatic behavioral success-responses.

The world is filled with people *who do not*

know how to direct and control their own lives. So they settle for their dull daily routines of mediocrity. It is a pity. *So much waste!*

But it is their own fault. They have not learned *how* their life-control system works, *so they do not control their lives but let their lives control them.*

They do not get what *they* want. They meekly accept whatever life doles out to them, and it is not much.

Yet the method of personally controlling life-guidance has been known for thousands of years. It has been taught by every religion. It has been taught by all of the wisest men who ever lived. It has been recorded since man learned to write. It is the most published fact of recorded thought.

The Bible states it so clearly: *"As a man thinketh, so IS he."*

Modern science has been able to add little to this profound, fundamental truth. The most important scientific addition has been the discovery by psychologists that *all people think in mental pictures.*

So psychologists now teach: *"People have a self-image (mental picture of themselves) and BECOME what they envision (mentally picture) themselves to be."*

Nothing could be clearer than that. Nothing could be more definite, more certain.

Proof is everywhere.

The rich (or would-be rich) "think rich"; they have *constant mental pictures* of wealth . . . and so *"the rich get richer".*

Look about you. The proof is everywhere!

The poor (and the uninformed) "think poor";

they have *constant mental pictures* of poverty . . . and so "the poor (and uninformed) get poorer".

Look about you. The proof is everywhere!

Yet this does not have to be. The poor do not have to "*think poor*" and visualize *constant mental pictures of poverty.* The *uninformed* do not have to remain *uninformed* and continue to *mentally picture* themselves as lacking opportunities—*because opportunities to succeed are as near as this book!*

Everyone can control his or her own thoughts (mental pictures), or can easily learn to control them.

The methods are simple and easy to understand. They are easy to use.

For example, the lesson of this chapter and several following chapters is that you must *dominate*—virtually *overwhelm*—your subconscious with the *intensity* and *constancy* of your mental pictures.

Here's why:

Your subconscious is literally bombarded with countless sensorium stimuli, thoughts, impulses, memory-recalls, and responses, in addition to the complex operation of your physical-mental life functions—most of which take place beyond your level of consciousness, so that you are unaware of them.

You cannot expect to *impress* your engrossed subconscious with only a *vague, infrequent, indifferent, indistinct mental picture of your life-goal.*

And you cannot expect your subconscious to disregard the enormous, countless pressures upon it, and to give an infrequent, indifferent, indistinct mental picture of your life-goal *top priority.* Certainly not!

Your subconscious which, cybernetically, is your life-guidance system, is not going to be any more impressed with the importance of your attaining your life-goal than YOU are.

This is the rule:

Your subconscious will use its unlimited power to *guide you to*, or to *attract to you*, WHATEVER you want—*in direct proportion* to the *intensity* and *frequency* of your *mental pictures of your actually possessing whatever you want.*

For example:

If you want to attain great wealth, you must *intensely* and *frequently* project into your life-guiding subconscious *vivid, impressive mental pictures* of your actually possessing great wealth.

To re-state this in terms of proved psychological research: If you constantly hold in your imagination a *self-image* (mental picture of yourself) possessing great wealth, you will BECOME what you *envision* (mentally picture) yourself to be: a possessor of great wealth.

Your self-image (mental picture) must be *"real"* in your *imagination.*

For your self-image (mental picture) to be *"real"* in your *imagination,* it must be so *intense* that it *dominates* your constant thought and, therefore, *dominates your life-guidance instructions to your subconscious.*

There are a number of psychological methods which will enable you to achieve such intense concentration that you can literally *computerize* your subconscious so that its *constant, principal objective* will be to *guide you to* or *attract to you* the opportunities, personal contacts, financial resources, knowledge and *whatever you need to attain your goal.*

There are psychological *concentration* methods which will keep your mind *intensely* focused on your goal over long spans of time not possible otherwise.

The following psychological concentration methods are especially recommended:

The *"Silent Chant"* Method
The *"Knotted Rope"* Method
The *"Magic Coins"* Method
The *"Repeating Card"* Method
The *"Self-Hypnosis"* Method

There is not space in this book to explain and teach these methods. An entire section of my book *How To Get Whatever You Want* is devoted to enabling *anyone* to learn and *start using* each powerful psychological method *in a few minutes.*

The book you now are reading will teach you *other* methods of directing your all-powerful subconscious.

There is a highly effective way to *intensify your mental picture* so that it will be your *constant, dominant thought*—which means that all of your principal thinking will relate directly or indirectly to it.

This method is called: GOAL COMMAND.

It is simple and easy to do, and it *greatly intensifies your mental pictures*—to enable you to *succeed faster!*

You will learn how to do it . . . in the next chapter . . .

Chapter 14

Here's HELP! . . .

Intensify Your Mental Pictures With A Forceful GOAL COMMAND!

As explained in preceding chapters, your subconscious is totally engrossed in the 24-hour-a-day operation of your physical-mental life functions and is subjected to sensorium stimuli beyond calculation!

So, if you tip-toe up to your subconscious with a *weak, inconsequential mental picture* of some indefinite life-goal, your subconscious will give you the *"I'm busy, boy, don't bother me"* treatment. And justifiably!

To impress your subconscious with your emphatic instructions to guide you to, or attract to you, what you want, *you must virtually overwhelm your subconscious with almost constant and very intense mental pictures of what you want.*

You have to "come on strong"! Take command! *Dominate your subconscious!*

And you can do this only by *frequent* (almost

constant), *very intense, extremely vivid mental pictures* of what you *command* your subconscious to materialize in your life.

This means using forceful, dominant personal power which will command the attention and compliance of your subconscious *to concentrate on your life-goal.*

Remember, your subconscious is unfeeling. It is a servo-mechanism. It only serves and produces. *It produces in direct proportion to the compelling power of the instructions it receives.*

So . . . your subconscious will produce what you want in *direct proportion* to the *intensity* and *frequency* of the *mental pictures* through which it envisions and understands what you want it to produce in your life.

Therefore, you must do everything possible to *greatly intensify* your *mental pictures* of what you want.

Here's HELP! . . .

You can *greatly intensify* your *mental pictures* with a forceful GOAL COMMAND which emphasizes *with words* what you are *mentally picturing*—and does so simultaneously.

The word-slogan GOAL COMMAND method is taught in complete detail in my 71-chapter book: *How To Get Whatever You Want.* You will benefit greatly by learning the complete method from that book.

However, I shall repeat part of it here so that you can use it to greatly intensify your mental picture instructions to your subconscious.

We have space here only for one example of a GOAL COMMAND. My book, *How To Get Whatever You Want,* gives many examples of word-slogan GOAL

COMMANDS for many life-goals, and explains how to create the most successful ones.

The example of a GOAL COMMAND which we shall use here is the GOAL COMMAND to your subconscious for it to produce *a life-goal of great wealth for worthy purposes.*

You would use the GOAL COMMAND to your subconscious: *"Make a million!"*

You would repeat this GOAL COMMAND silently—but *very forcefully*—to your subconscious at every opportunity, and this means *hundreds,* even *thousands* of times a day, continuously while bathing, shaving, dressing, during all waiting periods and during the *hundreds of daily opportunities* when you have the *two seconds* required for *each* repetition:

"Make a million!" . . . *"Make a million!"* . . . *"Make a million!"* . . . *"Make a million!"* . . . *"Make a million!"* (Repeat it mentally, over and over, at every opportunity. It requires only *two seconds* for *each* repetition.)

Now, use that GOAL COMMAND *"Make a million!"* to emphasize *your intense mental pictures* of your amassing great wealth, being a millionaire, using your great fortune to acquire *whatever you want* and *have almost unlimited means of helping others.*

See how much more compelling the combination of *intense mental pictures* emphasized by *forceful* GOAL COMMANDS is in *commanding* your subconscious to guide you to, or attract to you, what you want in life!

The *"Make a million!"* combination of *intense mental pitcures* emphasized by *forceful* GOAL COMMANDS has been used only as one example.

Appropriate mental pictures and *matching* GOAL COMMANDS can be used to *command* your subconscious to produce WHATEVER YOU WANT . . . *happiness! . . . love! . . . success! . . . wealth! . . . influence! . . . power! . . . popularity! . . . fame! . . . whatever you want!*

Now let us continue to discover more and more ways to *greatly INTENSIFY your mental picture instructions* to your subconscious which is your life-guidance system.

We shall add a highly effective—and *very exciting*—MENTAL PICTURE INTENSIFIER . . . in the next chapter . . .

Chapter 15

Here's HELP! . . .

Put EXCITEMENT Into Your Mental Pictures ... And Into Your Life!

The *more you impress* your subconscious with your mental picture and GOAL COMMAND to produce *what you want*—the *faster* you will get it.

In the preceding chapter we added the emphasis of using a forceful GOAL COMMAND to "verbalize" your *mental picture* so that your subconscious would mentally "*hear*" in addition to mentally "*seeing*" what you want as your life-goal.

It is a primary function of your subconscious to operate as your life-guidance system. But it can guide you *only* if you give it clear, forceful commands in *very intense* mental pictures.

Your subconscious must mentally "*see*" what you want—and what it "*sees*" must be *clear, vivid* and *intense*.

To further emphasize your intense mental picture, you must also "verbalize" your mental picture with a brief, concise, forceful GOAL COMMAND, repeated during *hundreds* of *two-second* opportunities during every day and night.

Thus, simultaneously, your subconscious will mentally *"see"* and mentally *"hear"* your goal-command.

Now . . . add a third mental dimension: *"mental emotion"* . . . EXCITEMENT!

Your subconscious, like your total personality, *is not activated by dullness.*

You cannot *activate* others by being dull, unenthusiastic, apathetic.

You cannot *activate* your own personality by being dull, unenthusiastic, apathetic.

And you cannot activate your subconscious with dull, unenthusiastic, apathetic mental pictures.

So get EXCITED about what you want!

Get EXCITED about your life-goal!

You *think* with *mental pictures*. That is what your *thoughts* are: *mental pictures.*

That is what your subconscious accepts as your *mental command* to guide your life: *mental pictures of what you want!*

So . . . *activate* your *mental pictures* with EXCITEMENT by being *excited about your life-goal!*

Excitement is contagious! *Excitement* will spread throughout your personality, transforming dullness (if you should have any) into radiance, even brilliance!

Excitement will do that same thing for your *mental pictures of your life-goal!*

And when you put *excitement* into your *mental*

59

pictures of your GOAL COMMAND to your subconscious, your subconscious gets highly excited (more properly, "*goal-activated*") in guiding you to, or attracting to you, *whatever is required* to materialize your life-goal into reality.

Excitement is a terrific activator!

Excitement stirs emotions!

When you put excitement into your voice, people pay instant attention.

When you develop an exciting personality, people become interested in you; if you are dull, they pass you by.

Excitement motivates *enthusiasm*—and the two together can work miracles in your life!

Then add the magnetic power of *expectation!*

Be *excited* about your life-goal!

Be *enthusiastic* about your plans and efforts to attain your life-goal!

Confidently *expect* to attain your life-goal!

"As a man *thinketh*, so IS he", says the Bible.

And . . . as a man *excitedly thinks—EX-CITEDLY, ENTHUSIASTICALLY EXPECTS*—so IS he . . . *quicker!*

Chapter 16

CONSTANTLY Repeat Your Goal Command To Your Subconscious!

What is it worth to you to *get whatever you want?*

What is it worth to you to become exactly the kind of person you want to be: *your ideal self?*

What is it worth to you to attain your *life-goal?*

Consider what those things are worth to you— because you have to pay a price for them.

The price of *getting whatever you want . . .* and *becoming whatever you want to be . . .* and *attaining your life-goal* is:

CONSTANTLY repeat your goal command in *exciting, intense mental pictures* emphasized by a simultaneous, forceful *word command.*

The success of using goal commands to your subconscious *depends* upon your mentally *repeating* them CONSTANTLY.

Of course, when I use the word "CON-STANTLY", it is for emphasis. Obviously, you have other matters which require your thought, so "CONSTANTLY" cannot be total, and I use it to mean *"every moment which is not absolutely required for other thought"*.

Perhaps the best way to explain just how CONSTANTLY you can impress your goal command into your subconscious, is to describe how I do it, myself.

First, let me assure you that I find the time to do this during a very busy life, consisting of research, writing books, writing nationally syndicated newspaper articles, writing national magazine articles, operating a substantial publishing business including all of its national advertising and marketing, managing my own and several other financial estates including the M. R. Kopmeyer Foundation, a perpetual charitable trust fund. And I try to reply personally to some of the voluminous correspondence resulting from having several million readers.

So I have to work until past midnight, seven days a week.

Then, how do I have the time to CON-STANTLY impress my own personal goal command into my subconscious?

Again, please remember that I am using the word "CONSTANTLY" in this method only in a relative sense—*not "total" but implying "so frequent as to be predominant in anyone's daily thought."* This is called *"subconscious saturation"* or *"goal command re-emphasis"*.

This is how I do it, myself:

I have *concentrated* my goal command so that it requires *only 2 seconds*. I urge you to do the same. If your goal command requires more than 2 seconds, it probably is too long. If it requires more than 3 seconds, it *is* too long.

My own goal-command is *concentrated into 4 words* (actually *less* than 2 seconds). A goal-command of *more than 8 words is too long*—for many obvious reasons.

When you compose your own goal command, concentrate "what you want" into a forceful *goal slogan* of 3 to 6 words which describe your goal (just as "Make a million!" is a forceful goal command to emphasize mental pictures of acquiring wealth).

Then your own 3-to-6 word goal command will require only 2 to 3 seconds for every repetition.

Now, let's see how CONSTANTLY (or how many times) you can impress a 2-second goal command into your subconscious every day.

Let's try it, using as an example a few of many intervals available in my own busy day:

I devote 20 minutes every day to planned, systematic physical conditioning: isometric exercises, weight lifting, etc. Because the exercises are routine and physical, I can use that 20 minutes to impress my goal command into my subconscious. My 2-second goal command can be mentally repeated *600 times* during my 20 minutes of physical conditioning every day.

Then I devote 20 minutes every day to mental conditioning which consists exclusively of repeating my goal command, using the intense concentration methods taught in my 71-chapter book *How To Get Whatever You Want:*

(1) The *"Silent Chant"* Method

(2) The *"Knotted Rope"* Method

(3) The *"Magic Coins"* Method

(4) The *"Deck of Cards"* Method

(5) The *"Mental Picture"* Method

(6) The *"Repeating Card"* Method

(7) The *"Self-Hypnosis"* Method

The simple use of these intense concentration methods is taught in detail in my book *How To Get Whatever You Want* so I need not take space here to describe them in detail.

I do not use all seven methods every day, but use about three of the foregoing intense concentration methods each day and rotate them for variety and sustained interest.

During my daily 20 minutes of mental conditioning using my 2-second goal command, I can impress my goal command into my subconscious an additional *600 times.*

So during my 20-minute *physical conditioning* and my 20-minute *mental conditioning periods* every day, I can impress my 2-second goal command into my subconscious *1,200 times!*

Then during 40 minutes a day devoted to the routine of shaving, bathing, dressing and grooming, which do not require mental concentration, I can impress *another 1,200* goal commands into my subconscious.

That makes a total of 2,400 goal commands every day!

Then add driving time and waiting time, and add the literally *hundreds* of brief time-periods not required for concentrated thought, and *you have a potential of impressing your own 2-second goal command into your subconscious more than 10,000 times every day!* No matter how busy you are!

To be realistic, let us assume that a person has a short attention span, weak mental concentration, and is easily distracted to wandering chains of "day-dream" thoughts. So his or her mental concentration on a specific goal command is only 10% efficient. *That still would mean 1,000 goal commands impressed into the subconscious every day!*

And even this 10% mental concentration efficiency is "CONSTANT" enough to *dominate the subconscious* with 1,000 goal commands every day!

When you dominate your subconscious with 1,000 or more goal commands every day—goal commands of exciting, intense mental pictures emphasized by 2-second, forceful word commands—you ASSURE *your attainment of any life-goal which you can conceive and believe.*

Of course, it is necessary that *you actually USE the countless opportunities, situations, personal contacts and the almost unlimited means of achieving your goal* which your subconscious will guide you to, or attract to you, in its cybernetic response to your goal command *which you have made its dominant objective* by methods taught in this chapter.

When you DO this, then expect the unexpected.

Seemingly miraculous and wonderful things will begin to happen in your life!

Chapter 17

Here's HELP! . . .

You Cannot Make A Picture
Without EXPOSURE!

Just as you cannot take a picture with your camera unless you EXPOSE the film to whatever *you want in your picture*—you cannot make a MENTAL PICTURE unless you EXPOSE YOUR MIND to whatever *you want to mentally picture*.

As you learned in the first part of this book, *your thoughts are mental pictures.*

Your mental pictures (thoughts which you consistently and intensely hold in your mind) are permanently recorded in your subconscious which is your life-guidance system.

And, as explained in the first part of this book, *your subconscious actually produces in your real life whatever you consistently and intensely mentally picture.*

The Bible teaches: "As a man THINKETH, so IS he." Your THOUGHTS are *mental pictures.*

And Buddha taught: "ALL that we ARE is the result of what we have THOUGHT."

Marcus Aurelius taught: "Our LIFE is what our THOUGHTS make it."

And William James reaffirmed eighteen centuries later: "Belief (confident THOUGHT) *creates the actual fact.*"

So your mental pictures (consistently and intensely held thoughts) are of great consequence to you—because *they will become your life!*

Your mind is like a camera.

Your mind makes *mental pictures* of *whatever* is EXPOSED to it.

And those *mental pictures* will subsequently become *your life!*

The lesson is clear and simple:

EXPOSE to your mind whatever you want in life. Your mind-camera will make a mental picture of *whatever* is exposed to it:

(a) *Actual objects:* If you want to be *rich,* EXPOSE to your mind *objects* related to *wealth:* money (use the "Dollar Bill Book Mark" described in a later chapter); make a *scrap-book* of pictures cut from magazines, pictures of expensive automobiles, luxury homes, fine furniture, expensive clothes, valuable jewelry, whatever represents *wealth* to *you.* Browse through your scrap-book frequently to EXPOSE your mind to objects of wealth. EXPOSE your mind to *worthy objectives of wealth;* visualize how you will use your wealth to help others.

(b) *Related activities:* Continuing our example of *mental picture* EXPOSURE to *wealth:* deposit money *every week* in a savings account. Buy growth stocks, even in limited amounts. If you cannot afford to actually buy stocks, make a list of ten stocks you would buy if you could. List the purchase price of each at the time of your imaginary investment. Follow their fluctuations *daily* in the stock price quotations in your newspaper. Subscribe to the leading financial publication and read it thoroughly. Consistently EXPOSE your mind to finance, money, wealth.

(c) *Personal contacts:* Still continuing our example of *mental picture* EXPOSURE to *wealth:* Know the *top* executives of your bank *personally.* If you do not now know them, introduce yourself. You are a customer of the bank. You have a right to know the executives. Meet and know the leading business executives in your city. If you can associate with them, by all means do so. But at least know them. Join organizations of successful people—especially those engaged in actively helping others.

The preceding examples are only a few of hundreds of ways you can consistently make *mental picture* EXPOSURES of *wealth,* which we used as an example.

Of course, you may not be interested in being wealthy. Certainly, there are more worthy life-goals (but wealth often is a useful resource in attaining many other goals). Choose *your* goal; you can attain *any* goal by using PROVEN SUCCESS METHODS.

But, *whatever* your life-goal, you must consistently and intensely hold in your mind *mental pictures* of the kinds of objects, activities and people related to it.

And the *only* way you can make a *picture*—with a camera or *in your mind*—is by EXPOSURE.

However, *camera* pictures require only an *instant* of EXPOSURE—but *mental-pictures* require CONSTANT EXPOSURE.

You must *constantly* project into your subconscious—a continuous flow of *mental pictures* produced by *consistent* EXPOSURE to objects, activities, associates, ideas, thoughts, plans and everything *related to what you want as your life-goal*.

Note that your EXPOSURE must be *consistent* with your life-goal. You cannot EXPOSE your mental camera to activities and thoughts associated with *failure*—and expect it to produce mental pictures of *success* to guide your subconscious.

You must be *deliberately selective* in choosing the associates, the activities, the reading, and everything to which you EXPOSE your mind, *because each and every EXPOSURE will be a mental picture* . . . and each mental picture will guide your life to be *consistent* with the EXPOSURE.

For as the world-famous psychologist-writer-preacher, Dr. Norman Vincent Peale, says: "When the MENTAL PICTURE or attitude is strongly enough held, it actually seems to CONTROL CONDITIONS AND CIRCUMSTANCES."

You'd better believe it!

Chapter 18

Here's HELP! . . .

EXPOSE Your Mental Camera To Hundreds Of Success Opportunities!

The preceding chapter introduced you to the need for EXPOSURE to make *mental pictures* of what you want.

Why do you need mental pictures of what you want?

Because your subconscious will use your mental pictures: (a) to guide you to, or (b) to attract to you— *whatever you mentally picture.*

The PROVEN SUCCESS METHOD is to constantly *flood* your subconscious with mental pictures of *your succeeding in getting what you want.*

For brevity, we shall simply call your succeeding in getting what you want: "success".

So what this chapter is about is: EXPOSING YOURSELF TO SUCCESS!

The more you expose yourself to success, the

more opportunities you will have to become successful—and the *faster* you will succeed!

In my book, *How To Get Whatever You Want,* I emphasized that you will greatly speed up your success by actively making and maintaining contacts with *successful people* who have influence, money and a wide range of "success contacts" of their own.

In the words of the financial counselors, *"Go where the success and money is!"*

EXPOSE your mind to success opportunities! Go in person . . . go by mail . . . go by telephone . . . but GO!

You've got to get up . . . get out . . . and get among 'em! Give your mind SUCCESS EXPOSURE!

If you want to eliminate forever *your* fear of failure—EXPOSE your mental camera to *hundreds* of possible success opportunities! Keep a *continuous flow* of mental pictures of success *literally flooding your subconscious.*

You cannot expect your subconscious to be greatly impressed by your intense (?) desire to attain your life-goal if *only occasionally* you send it an indifferent mental picture of it. *Remember, your subconscious is receiving mental pictures of something every few seconds!*

So, if only one out of a hundred of the mental pictures which your subconscious receives is of your life-goal, your subconscious will not consider that occasional mental picture as a dynamic goal command!

Your subconscious will respond only to the exact degree of *frequency* and *intensity* of your mental pictures of what you want as your life-goal.

If you are aimless and indifferent in thinking

about your life-goal, your subconscious will be equally aimless and indifferent in directing you to your goal or in attracting what you want.

But if you EXPOSE your mind to every conceivable success opportunity . . . if you mentally keep your success "production line" filled with opportunities moving toward your life-goal . . . if you flood your subconscious with *consistent, constant, intense* mental pictures of success . . . you will activate the vast power of your subconscious to materialize those *consistent, constant, intense* mental pictures into reality.

Your subconscious *has the power*—as part of the *Infinite Mind*, it has *infinite power*—but *you* must furnish the *goal command* and the *motivation* through mental pictures made by EXPOSING your mind to every possible success opportunity you can imagine, read about, or see in real life.

Fill your subconscious with mental pictures of success—and your subconscious will fill your life with success!

Chapter 19

Here's HELP! . . .

Make A CONSTANT COMPANION
Of Your Ideal Self-Image

As stated in preceding chapters, modern psychology in recent tests again has confirmed that: *"People have a self-image and become what they envision (mentally picture) themselves to be."*

This leads to several obvious but very important conclusions:

(1) That you NOW already have or are presently forming a *self-image (mental picture)* of a FUTURE YOU which *you definitely will become*—for better or for worse—depending on the *kind* of FUTURE YOU which you mentally picture.

(2) You had better IMAGINE the *best possible self-image*—the mental picture of a FUTURE YOU which *you really want to become*—because that is what *you will be in the future.*

(3) You should start now to *begin becoming* that IDEAL YOU which you mentally picture as your *best self-image*.

How?

The most stimulating and effective way is to *make a CONSTANT COMPANION of your ideal self-image*.

No, it isn't difficult. In fact, it is easy.

Here's how:

First, you must decide what you want to be in the future.

If you cannot decide *exactly* what you want to be—then *imagine* the BEST YOU which you can mentally picture.

Make *that* your *ideal self-image*—what you want to become. Practice, by *imagining*, until you can *"see"* yourself in your *imagination*—*clearly* as you *want* to be.

Now, *imagine* that your *ideal self-image* is your *constant companion* . . . your *invisible friend* . . . your *helpful advisor*.

Imagine a *clear* mental picture of your *ideal self-image* (your BEST YOU)—so that, *in your imagination*, you can mentally picture YOU *at your future best*.

Make it *mentally real*. Think of this BEST YOU as an *invisible, constant companion* . . . it must never leave you . . . always be near you . . . all day . . . all night . . . your *constant companion* . . . your *invisible friend* . . . your *helpful advisor*.

Now you have the BEST YOU—the IDEAL YOU which you want to become—always with you *in your imagination*—as a constant ideal to strive to be like . . . as a companion, friend, advisor.

Advisor? How can an *imaginary* mental picture *advise* you?

That is the best part. You no longer have to make decisions—sometimes very serious decisions—*alone.*

You talk them over—*mentally,* of course, with your *ideal self-image* . . . the BEST YOU . . . the IDEAL YOU *which you are gradually (or rapidly) becoming.*

You mentally ask, "What would my IDEAL SELF do in this situation?"

Then you decide and act always in accordance with the wisest, noblest, finest advice of the BEST YOU, the IDEAL YOU which you want to become.

You always follow the choice or the decision which the BEST YOU, the IDEAL YOU *would* make.

As a psychiatrist would advise, *"Always live up to the ideals of your finest self-image."*

This sets up a mental block against any temptations to be, act, or associate with, less than the BEST in terms of your finest IDEAL.

This is the most effective method of personality development and character building.

When perfected to the highest mental state in which your imaginary self-image of the BEST YOU, the IDEAL YOU becomes a *"real"* (although invisible) *constant companion, friend* and *advisor*—you will have the inspiring sensation of being part of a miracle!

It is then that you and your ideal self-image merge into one—and you will have become your IDEAL YOU!

"People *become* what they *mentally picture* themselves to *be.*"

Chapter 20

Here's HELP! . . .

Why You Must MASTER Problems, Problem-People And Yourself

Let us begin with the most obvious answers:

(1) Either you master your problems or your problems will master you.

(2) Either you master problem-people or they will control you. It is a distinctive characteristic of problem-people that they will resort to almost any means to control others.

(3) Either you master yourself or you will find yourself causing most of your own problems in addition to causing problems of others, often those nearest and dearest to you.

Well, those obvious reasons should be reasons enough for you to master problems, problem-people and yourself.

But most problems and their causes are not obvious at all. They lurk, hidden in your subconscious, to combine in devious ways to confront you suddenly with problems you did not even know you had!

Then there is the propensity of problems, like cancer cells, to multiply until their growth overwhelms us.

The earth literally is filling up with people who are being completely overwhelmed by the devastating multiplicity of problems!

Problems rapidly beget more problems. We have less to fear from a "population explosion" than we do from the much more imminent *"problem explosion"*.

Here's HELP! . . .

It is the purpose of this book—not to *eliminate* problems (which cannot be done)—but to provide you with the methods and the power to *master problems* as they confront you; to *master problem-people* who would disrupt your life; to *master yourself*—as part of *becoming* the kind of *ideal person* you want to be.

You cannot accomplish these most desirable objectives *just by reading this book.*

You *must* do the following:

(1) Re-read . . . and re-read . . . and re-read this book until its *proven success methods* become your instant *thought-responses* and *emotional-responses* to every situation and event.

It is the purpose of this book to *pre-condition* your responses so that *whatever* happens, you *instantly* and *automatically* will react (or *not* react, or *not* OVER-react) *so that you will be effective and successful.*

(2) *Constantly* USE the *proven success methods* in this and my other books. *Only by USING proven success methods* can you possibly succeed.

Chapter 21

Here's HELP! . . .

Keep A QUIET MIND

This is one of the most important lessons in becoming your IDEAL SELF:

Keep a QUIET MIND.

This is the *only* way to solve your problems
calmly, intelligently, logically:

Keep a QUIET MIND.

This is the *only* way to maintain *mental command* over problem-people—no matter how insulting, no
matter how arrogant, no matter how hostile they are:

Keep a QUIET MIND.

This is the *only* way to manage a situation in
which anger flames, tempers flare and inflammatory emotions threaten to burn part of your life to ashes:

Keep a QUIET MIND.

This is what Kipling meant when he wrote
*". . . keep your head when all about you are losing theirs—
and blaming it on you".*

Keep a QUIET MIND.

When others yell and shout and rant and rave in their stupid efforts to overwhelm by sheer noise what they cannot solve by sensible thought—let them exhaust their emotions by their verbal assaults against the always impenetrable wall of silence. Bide your time and patiently wait out the noisy storm no matter how long it takes, and meanwhile:

Keep a QUIET MIND.

In becoming a *Positive Power* ($\times$ +) *Person,* your first step to power—*the power to manage yourself so that you can manage others and, subsequently, even manage circumstances* (as you will learn in other chapters) is:

Keep a QUIET MIND.

A QUIET MIND in a crisis is like the *"eye"* of a hurricane. In a hurricane, destructive winds whirl violently—except in the center (the *"eye"*) of the hurricane which is a place of *absolute calm* in the very center of the destructive forces all around it.

By an amazing coincidence, *your own eyes* must be like the *"eyes"* of hurricanes—because in every emotional storm, *your own eyes* must be the center of *absolute calm.*

Because it is the *absolute calm of your relaxed eyes* which is the unusual (*and perhaps astonishing*) method of keeping a QUIET MIND—you will learn *how to control your mind-moods (emotions) by eye-relaxation* . . . in the next chapter . . .

Chapter 22

Here's HELP! . . .

A QUIET MIND Begins With Relaxing Your EYE-Emotions

There is a very close relationship between your eyes and your mind.

This action-reaction between your eyes and your mind includes but is very much greater than *physical* vision.

Your eyes are highly emotional. *They respond to emotion and they stimulate or they relax your mind-moods (emotions).*

This is beyond physical vision (*"outer vision"*).

Eye-emotion directly affects *"inner vision"* (mental pictures and mind-moods). Therefore, it is important that you learn to *control your eye-emotions.*

First, let us consider how your eyes *respond* to your mind-moods (emotions).

Your eyes *weep* in grief; your eyes *smolder* with resentment; your eyes *flash* with anger; your *eyes flame* with hostility. And when they do, they *not only respond* to your emotions, but they *stimulate* and *escalate* the emotions to which they *respond*—and which they *openly express.*

By relaxing the intensity of your eye-emotions, you can calm the mind-moods (emotions), themselves, and take the first step toward achieving a QUIET MIND.

Eye-control of mind-moods is accomplished by:

(1) Your becoming *consciously aware* of the emotion which *your eyes are expressing*—realizing that tense eye-emotion *stimulates* and *escalates* the *mind-mood itself* (in accordance with the action-reaction principle taught by famed psychologist William James of Harvard).

Conscious awareness enables you to *focus on your emotion* so that you can relax it with the restraint of mind control induced by eye relaxation.

(2) RELAX YOUR EYES! You can relax your eyes simply by *mental command*—by deliberately causing your eyes to *feel relaxed.* "Blank-out" all eye-tension. Make your eyes *"feel blank."* Imagine your eyes having a "blank look." Unemotional. Unresponsive. Blank. Completely relaxed. Almost asleep.

When your eyes are *completely relaxed*—they absolutely *cannot* stimulate, escalate—*or even sustain*—violent, uncontrolled emotions of resentment, anger, hate, hostility, anxiety, fear, panic or any turbulent, high-tension emotion.

It is psychologically impossible for you to feel two directly opposite emotions at the same time.

So by *completely relaxing your eyes* and "blanking-out" all eye-emotions, you *"turn off"* the high-tension, self-damaging emotions of resentment, anger, hate, anxiety, fear and panic.

This, like so much of life, is controlled by the universal *Law of Consistency.*

If your eyes smolder with resentment, your mind-mood also will be resentful. If your eyes flash with anger, your mind-mood also will burn with anger.

Your emotions always will be the same (consistent) throughout your entire nerve system.

For that same reason (*consistency*), by RELAXING YOUR EYES, *you relax your mind-mood* so that you *cannot feel tense.*

And because you cannot feel tense, you cannot feel—or express—high-tension emotions of resentment, anger, hate, anxiety, fear and panic.

You simply *"turn off"* tense emotions when you RELAX YOUR EYES.

So, whenever you begin to feel tense, RELAX YOUR EYES!

You will feel *physically* relaxed.

You will feel *mentally-emotionally* relaxed.

You will achieve *one of life's most rewarding and satisfying attainments* . . . a QUIET MIND.

Chapter 23

Here's HELP! ...

To Keep A QUIET MIND ...
Do Not Emotionalize Trouble

It is the purpose of this chapter, not to deny or belittle the existence of trouble, but to offer some helpful suggestions for dealing with trouble realistically.

So let us first admit that there is trouble, that trouble comes to us frequently and in varying amounts, and that we cannot prevent it.

Therefore we must learn to accept trouble and sometimes to live amid troubles—*without being overwhelmed by them.*

For it is our own fault if we allow ourselves to be overwhelmed by the difficulties, the troubles, the tragedies of life.

When I was a very young man, I read in a publication of that half-century ago, these words which I have remembered ever since: "Life is real; Life is earnest; *but you don't have to get 'red in the neck' about it!*"

It is the excitable, emotional, trouble-sensitive people who find something wrong in everything and get "red in the neck" in their frenzied, annoying efforts to set everything right at once. Or they stew inwardly until their emotions are a seething, bubbling, boiling mess.

It would help us to deal with trouble if we understood what trouble really is. Trouble is neither a reward nor a punishment; trouble simply is a consequence.

Being a consequence, trouble may be avoided by avoiding its cause. This often is possible. But if some trouble cannot be foreseen or cannot be avoided—so be it. Trouble will arrive and will have to be dealt with.

The first and constant requirement is: DO NOT EMOTIONALIZE TROUBLE!

By emotionalizing trouble, we over-emphasize it, whatever its nature. If we do not emotionalize trouble, our degree of difficulty with it becomes merely a means of measurement which states the amount of physical, mental and spiritual effort required to surmount it. Then our difficulty with trouble has no more significance than a yardstick. Trouble can grow in significance only as we emotionalize it.

We intensify trouble by complaining about it. "We protest too much," Shakespeare would say.

Every scratch on the hand is not a stab in the heart. So let us not emotionalize it. We have merely been scratched; we have not been stabbed. Our sensitive feelings have been hurt more than our person.

People go about moaning that their cup of misfortune overfloweth, when it is not even full! They make up in emotion what they do not really have in misfortune.

Most troubles usually are not as bad as they seem. They couldn't be! Nevertheless, do not go into a thunderstorm of troubles, carrying a lightening rod in each hand. *Do not seek trouble. At least, make it find you.* It may, but it will take it longer!

And, when trouble does find you—as it may— *do not emotionalize it!* Be as impassively serene as Buddha, as resigned to the inevitable as a Stoic, as submissively patient as Job, as accepting in faith as a persecuted Christian. *Do not emotionalize trouble!*

Examine your trouble with the calm, reasoning judgment of a QUIET MIND.

Do not become any more emotionally involved with trouble than a modern psychiatrist listening to an emotionally disturbed patient who is confessing the most horrible impulses of suicide, mass murder, and the wildest, weirdest, abnormal conduct!

The psychiatrist listens attentively with all the surprise, alarm and excitement of being told what brand of cereal the patient ate for breakfast.

This does not mean that the psychiatrist is not intensely interested and deeply concerned; it means that the psychiatrist does not permit his own emotional involvement in his patient's already over-emotionalized problems to interfere with reasoned judgment.

Let us not allow our own emotions to transcend our reason. *Life is a varied, interesting experience to those who think, but often a tragedy to those who feel, not wisely, but too much.*

One way people emotionalize trouble is to have a temper tantrum. Temper affects you like a stimulant. A temper tantrum is like a convulsive fit; it makes you feel stronger for a brief time, but for long afterward you are weaker. You not only are weaker physically, but you are weaker mentally, emotionally and spiritually. For long afterward.

Each emotional outburst in response to any kind of trouble lowers your resistance to the next. Emotionalized trouble is like a large, round rock at the top of the stairs. Once it starts thudding downward, it cannot be stopped midway, but continues its disastrous descent until it hits emotional bottom—with a personality-shattering crash!

Trouble is sufficient unto itself and should not be escalated by emotion. Instead, trouble should be repaired with a gentle touch. *You cannot fix a damaged watch with a hammer.* You cannot repair the Timepiece of Life with hard blows, but rather by carefully regulating each minute so that the hours will be adjusted in harmony with the Master Clock of Eternity.

Chapter 24

Here's HELP! ...

To Keep A QUIET MIND ...
Do Not OVER-React

Most people think that their unhappiness, much or little, is caused by *what happens to them.*

Not so!

Unhappiness, also resentment, anger, anxiety, fear, and other unpleasant emotional disturbances are caused by how you *feel* about what happens.

So, you may or may not be the *initial* cause of your own (and others') unhappiness—but *you certainly are the principal cause.*

Because it is *how you feel* about whatever happens and *how you react* in response to your feeling—*which will be the direct and principal cause* of your own (and others') unhappiness, resentment, anger, anxiety, fear and other unpleasant emotional disturbances.

Famed psychologist William James taught that *we can control our feelings by controlling our actions.*

That applies equally to our RE-actions, so let us concentrate on our reactions in seeking to remove this cause of our unhappiness and unpleasant emotions.

We react in one of four ways to every thought, sensation, situation or happening which reaches our consciousness.

(1) We OVER-react—ranging from relatively mild OVER-reaction to extreme OVER-reaction which may lead to our being *emotionally overwhelmed* (even to death resulting from heart failure).

(2) We INCONSISTENTLY react—which means that we react in a manner *opposite to normally expected prudent response.* Thus, we laugh at danger; we conspicuously ignore serious warnings; we contemptuously distain necessary help.

(3) We NON-react—that is, we simply do not respond or react at all.

(4) We react with the calm, thoughtful deliberation of a QUIET MIND.

The preceding descriptions of the four ways in which you may react to every thought, sensation, situation or happening—make it evident that *only two forms of reacting are compatible with success:* NON-reacting and reacting with the calm, thoughtful deliberation of a QUIET MIND.

Also, it is clear that INCONSISTENT reacting is abnormal, irrational or insane. If this form of response is usual, then personal therapy should be sought immediately.

So let us focus our attention on OVER-reaction to your *feelings* about the thoughts, sensations, situations and happenings which reach your attention.

The great French philosopher, Montaigne, wisely observed: "A man is not hurt so much by *what* happens to him—as by his *opinion* of what happens."

It is not *what* happens, but how *you feel about it*, which really matters to you.

So, remember, you OVER-react to your *feelings, themselves, not to whatever caused the feelings*.

Therefore, *OVER-reaction* is principally caused by *OVER-sensitive feelings*.

And it logically follows that the way to prevent OVER-reacting is to stop being OVER-sensitive.

This is easy and it will greatly benefit you throughout your entire life.

The way to stop being OVER-sensitive begins with *acceptance* of the fact that people, things, situations and events *are not perfect*.

Nor, are they provided for your personal approval or pleasure.

Nor, is it *your* responsibility to demand perfection or to personally attempt to make perfect an obviously imperfect world . . . filled with obviously imperfect people . . . creating obviously imperfect situations.

So *accept* the imperfections of others as you hope they will accept your own imperfections.

Do not be OVER-sensitive to imperfection, and you will not OVER-react to its frequent appearance.

Reality is a world full of people who are busy looking out for themselves and, in the process, may unintentionally jossle you about a bit. Nothing personal. It is just that others are preoccupied with their own problems and purposes.

Being preoccupied with their own problems, others are not particularly concerned about your own tender feelings.

That's how it is—*accept* it!

Do not be OVER-sensitive to imperfection. Do not OVER-react; it will either get you nowhere—or get you into trouble.

One day, Marcus Aurelius, one of the wisest of the ancient Roman rulers, wrote in his diary: "I am going to meet people today who talk too much—people who are selfish, egotistical, ungrateful. But *I will not be surprised or disturbed,* for I couldn't imagine a world without such people."

Now, centuries later, you are going to meet such people, too. So do not be OVER-sensitive to their imperfections and do not OVER-react in resentment, anger or hostility. *Accept* the fact that such people *do* exist, always have existed, always will.

Since no one has changed these facts of human behavior since the beginning of mankind, *you have not been designated as the one to do so now!*

So, relax . . . do not be OVER-sensitive to imperfection . . . do not get uptight about it . . . do not OVER-react in disapproval . . . develop the serene attitude of *acceptance* of what cannot be changed and . . .

Keep a QUIET MIND.

Chapter 25

Here's HELP! . . .

Do Not OVER-React In Resentment Or In Anger

I do not agree with Hans Habe, the German author who wrote: "The world is one percent good, one percent bad, *and ninety-eight percent neutral.*"

Well, this old world and its self-centered transient inhabitants are not all that *neutral!*

So, if you are OVER-sensitive, you can find plenty of real or imagined occasions to OVER-react in resentment—which usually escalates into anger.

This does no good—and great harm!

Resentment and anger—whether suppressed in a "slow burn" or exhibited in a convulsive temper-tantrum —exhaust you emotionally, physically, mentally and spiritually. *They exhaust you—and cost you!*

You lose respect and future opportunities of leadership.

People who OVER-react in resentment and

anger reveal that they are neurotic. The neurotic person is constantly being bruised by reality—and reacts in resentment and anger. As philosopher Marcus Aurelius wrote: "Anger is a mark of weakness; it means being hurt . . . and wincing."

Are you OVER-sensitive?

Are your tender feelings easily hurt?

Do you wince emotionally at every incidental offense?

Are you thin-skinned emotionally so that the slightest social "cut" becomes a deep, painful wound which festers into the spreading infection of resentment and anger?

And do you "rub salt in the wound" by constantly thinking about it?

Here's HELP! . . .

Get tough emotionally! No more OVER-sensitive feelings which "bleed" at the slightest scratch in this world filled with briars!

Use these two simple, but sure, methods:

(1) *Ignore it!* Marine General Smedley "Hell-Devil" Butler said he had been called every unprintable name there was! Did he feel "hurt"? Was "Old Hell-Devil" offended? Of course not! He said, "Whenever I hear someone cussing me, I never bother to turn my head to see who's talking."

Ignore it! General Eisenhower said he never wasted a minute thinking about people he didn't like.

But you don't have to be a General to be tough emotionally. You can be like quiet, distinguished Bernard Baruch, advisor to six Presidents of the United States. He said, "No man can humiliate me or disturb me. I won't let him."

And that's how to stop OVER-reaction in resentment and anger—*before it starts!* Paraphrase the calm, sure words of Bernard Baruch: *"Nothing* and *nobody* can disturb me. I won't *let* them."

How? Do not *let* them—simply by *ignoring* would-be disturbers.

Another way to avoid OVER-reacting in resentment and anger is, in the words of show business: *"Do not make a big production out of it."*

Do not make a mountain out of a molehill of some suspected, imaginary, or even real offense.

Be too big to be little!

But if you stupidly let some suspected, imaginary or even real offense get by your "emotional wall," use method number two:

(2) *Turn it off!*

Use the methods previously described in this book to *"relax your eyes"* and thus make it *"inconsistent"* to feel emotion of any kind. *Turn off your emotion.*

Thus, you will achieve a QUIET MIND which *nobody* and *nothing* can disturb.

While it is not within the province of this book to provide "peace which *passeth* understanding", it is a specific purpose of this book to enable its readers to attain and maintain *peace of mind* which is the *result of understanding.*

And to that end, let us take a closer look at one of the principal *disturbers of peace (of mind)* . . . RE-SENTMENT. In the next chapter . . .

Chapter 26

Here's HELP! . . .

Resentment Is Replaying
A Stacked Deck!

Resentment is replaying a losing hand of cards dealt from a stacked deck. The cards (events) already have been arranged by the past and cannot be reshuffled. The deck is stacked. *Resentment cannot win because it cannot rearrange the past and so continues to suffer by emotionally reliving a painful event which cannot be changed.*

Resentment is trouble in past tense.

Whatever caused your resentment *already has happened* and therefore *cannot be undone.*

Since the past cannot be changed, and the event cannot be altered, you are left with two options if you would alleviate the gnawing torture of resentment:

(1) *Change your attitude toward the cause of your resentment.* Remember, it is not *what* happens, but how you *feel* about what happens, which is all that matters.

(2) *Forget it!* Confucius taught, "To be

wronged is nothing—*unless you continue to remember it.*"

No situation can be improved by your resentment. It can only be made worse.

And you are twice the victim: first of the event, and then of your own resentment of it. The event will be lost in the diffusion of time. Your continuing resentment of it will remain a burning ulcer in your spirit.

Resentment usually is the first link in what becomes a chain of increasingly violent emotions.

Resentment leads to anger.

Anger leads to hate.

Hate leads to hostility.

Hostility leads to violence.

So, get rid of resentment before it leads to something worse.

Stop resentment at its source—by considering its source . . . *with sympathetic understanding.*

In many cases, you will find that the (often imagined) slurs, slights, rudeness or other annoyances which arouse your resentment *are not intentional at all,* but are caused by the very human trait of people being preoccupied with their own thoughts, plans and problems.

Anyway, always assume that every slight annoyance is not intentional—and completely IGNORE it!

Why?

Because your resentment never hurts the person against whom you harbor your resentment. *It hurts only you.* Why deliberately hurt yourself?

Remember, it is not *what* happens, but how you *feel* about what happens, which is all that matters.

The choice is yours.

You can stew in burning resentment.

You can *assume* that the offense was *unintentional*—and *ignore* it.

You can *shrug it off* as being too insignificant to deserve your attention.

Or, you can *laugh at it*—which will get rid of resentment instantly.

Yes, the choice is yours, but consider the advice which dates back to the first century, when Martial taught, *"Laugh—if you are wise."*

Laughter is your *declaration of superiority* over resentment—and the *cause* of the resentment.

Laugh . . . *then forget it!* Forget it . . . NOW!

Sooner or later, you are going to forget the minor annoyances which, today, cause you irritation and resentment.

So why let yourself get emotionally stirred up by some insignificant happening which you won't even remember a week from now . . . a month from now . . . a year from now?

It won't interfere with your happiness *then.* Why let it interfere with your happiness *now?*

Laugh . . . *then forget it!* . . . NOW!

Chapter 27

Here's HELP! . . .

Anger Is SELF-Poison

There is a scorpion in South America which, when angered, becomes so furious that it stings itself with its own poison and dies.

This is a fitting climax to anger, because anger is, indeed, SELF-poison.

This SELF-poison by our own anger has been warned against by the ancient philosophers. These warnings against anger have come ringing down through the centuries since the first recorded wisdom. Now the SELF-poison of anger has been scientifically documented by the research of modern psychology.

The ancient Greek philosopher, Pythagoras wrote, "Anger begins in folly and ends in repentance." Modern psychology would add that, while the anger often is openly and vehemently expressed, the repentance which follows is usually repressed and festers in various forms of self-guilt in our subconscious.

The backlash of our anger whips against our own feverish flesh and leaves scars which the future may never heal and which regret may never hide. As John Webster said, "There is not in nature a thing that makes a man so deformed, so beastly as does intemperate angery."

The English statesman and historian, the Earl of Clarendon, wrote, "Anger hurts the one who is possessed by it more than the one against whom it is directed." And so it does because anger is SELF-poison.

But let us not overlook the certainty that our anger also hurts others. And, in hurting others, makes them our enemies and arouses their anger against us.

Anger begets anger. Anger escalates until the situation has all the charm of a swarm of attacking wasps. And the temporary exhileration which comes from releasing emotion in the form of anger just isn't worth the eventual cost.

Anger disguised as wit or cleverness isn't funny. It is cruel and it is costly. As Francis Bacon wrote, "Anger makes dull men witty, but it keeps them poor." There is much profit in silence, but seldom so much as in the restraint to remain silent in the tempting moment. Clever remarks which hurt others for the sake of a moment's wit are bad enough, but when such cleverness conceals the cutting edge of anger, the wound seldom heals.

Heed the wisdom of the proverb: *"He who can suppress a moment's anger may prevent a day of sorrow."* And, modern psychiatrists will assure you that the resulting self-sorrow will last for much longer than a day. *It may last a lifetime!*

So, the "ounce of prevention" principle should

be applied to anger because, in the wise words of Tyron Edwards: "To rule one's anger is well; to prevent it is better."

For anger is like a storm at sea; the waves continue long after the tempest has subsided. The turbulence of anger cannot be quieted instantly by ceasing the provocation.

Temper tantrums will weaken your resistance to future outbursts of anger. Back in the first century, the Greek biographer, Plutarch, in his study and recording of the lives of his time, observed, "Frequent fits of anger produce a propensity to be angry and cause the mind to become peevish and wounded at the least occurrence."

You can get "high" on emotion (including the emotion of anger) just as you can get "high" on alcohol or drugs. The effect of an emotional "high" can be just as dangerous and as damaging as that of alcohol or drugs. The "hang-over" which follows is just as depressing and the possibility of getting "hooked" is just as real. In fact, if you have or acquire a propensity for anger, there is a strong probability that you will become an *"anger addict"*, and this may be as physically, mentally and emotionally dangerous as being an alcoholic or drug addict. *In its advanced stages, anger addiction is almost as difficult to cure as alcoholism and some forms of drug addiction.*

We shall consider later in this chapter some ways to deal with anger—your anger or that of others directed toward you. But, first, let us examine some relevant aspects of anger.

When a person is wrong and won't admit it, he often gets angry. But the flames of anger illuminate the error while they heat the branding-iron of guilt. Anger is a wrong and costly diversion, since a prompt and frank admission of error will dull the edge of criticism and win, if not admiration, at least sympathetic understanding.

Anger is used for emphasis in attracting attention. Today it is fashionable to be angry or, at least, to act and speak angrily. *Thus, the angry protestors who are willing to shout for almost any cause about which they can give vent to anger in a succession of emotional binges.*

One can judge their true character by their manner of speech. A speech is like the ringing of a bell. One can tell by the tone whether the speaker is cracked or not. The strident voices of hatred, today so familiar, reveal the fractured emotional stability of the shouters.

The heat of anger, the flames of passion, the fires of hatred have melted many an ersatz halo, leaving the wearer looking very silly, because nothing makes one look more ridiculous than wearing the wilted, dripping remnants of a melted halo.

Life is too brief to permit animosity, resentment or anger to add to our difficulties. *There is nothing to be gained by escalating trouble.*

So let us consider the preventatives and remedies for anger recommended by some of the wisest men of history. *"The greatest remedy for anger is delay,"* wrote Seneca. And Thomas Jefferson defined the delay: "When angry, count to ten before you speak; if very angry, count a hundred." This old and worn admonition has withstood the wear-test of frequent use.

Sydney Smith also recommended delay to cool anger, and writes from his own experience, "We are told,

'Let not the sun go down on your wrath,' but I would add, 'Never write or act until it has done so.' This rule has saved me from many an act of folly. It is wonderful what a different view we take of the same event four-and-twenty hours after it has happened."

And we thank Reverend Smith for that very good advice.

Speak softly, advised Solomon, whose very name is symbolic of wisdom: "A soft answer turneth away wrath, but grievous words store up anger."

In dealing with anger, we are dealing with an emotion which, like all other emotions, can be controlled. *Since all emotions are our own responses, we can control the intensity of our emotions by consciously controlling the degree of our own responses.* We can pre-condition ourselves not to OVER-react and, eventually not to respond adversely at all.

To laugh at provocation is to demolish it; then to forgive, is to forget it entirely.

The psychological "need to conquer" is as false as it is ineffective. *It is much safer to reconcile an enemy than to conquer him.* A reconciled enemy is no longer an enemy, but a conquered enemy remains an enemy still, and is all the more vindictive.

You can assign most of your duties to others, but only you can forgive your enemy.

And, only *you* can deal with an insult. There are three effective ways to treat an insult. The first is to ignore it. But if you cannot ignore it, then laugh at it. If you cannot laugh at it, it probably is deserved and you should learn from it.

Our antagonist is our teacher if we will but learn from him, not letting our emotions blind us from seeing lessons which our friends dare not try to teach. Throughout life, you will find that you will learn more and harder lessons from your enemies than from your friends.

So, even if you cannot love your enemies, do not hate them. Being adversaries, they exercise your initiative and develop your strength. Being provocators, they challenge your discipline to keep cool.

And, by keeping cool, you keep control . . . control over others . . . control over circumstances.

That is a condition worthy of your continuing efforts.

It is the QUIET MIND.

Chapter 28

Here's HELP! . . .

WORRY Is A Mental HORROR MOVIE! Turn It Off Before It Wrecks You!

In previous chapters, you learned that your thoughts really are *mental pictures* and, because your thoughts are a *continuous series* of mental pictures, you are constantly projecting a MENTAL MOVIE on the "picture screen" of your mind.

WARNING! . . .

When you *worry* you are impressing a mental HORROR MOVIE into your *subconscious!*

If you *continue to worry* you will be mentally watching—and subconsciously absorbing—*re-runs* of mental HORROR MOVIES . . . over . . . and over . . . and over . . . again!

The worry-plots of your mental HORROR MOVIES may vary, but their effect on *you* is the same.

Worry will tear you to pieces—emotionally, mentally and physically. *It will make you a human wreck.*

Do not put yourself through this *SELF-torture* in the mistaken belief that you are "thinking (with due concern) about your problems".

Worry is not "thinking"; worry is "emotionalizing". (If you were *thinking,* you would not be worrying.)

A *worry-tantrum* is like a temper-tantrum—only a *worry-tantrum* is much worse.

At least, a *temper-tantrum* may let some mental poison *out* (although mostly it reinforces it in your subconscious), but a *worry-tantrum pumps mental poison into your mind until it overflows throughout your entire being!* Result: frustration leading to nervous exhaustion.

Worry is a mental HORROR MOVIE of a *few* of the adversities which you are afraid *may* happen. (Note especially the words: *"few"* and *"may".*)

You can only worry about a *few* of the adversities which *may* happen, because life mercifully puts a limit on this kind of SELF-torture.

If you *could* and *did worry* about the *literally thousands* of adversities which actually *may* happen in your life, *you would go insane in a day!*

So you worry *selectively.* You *select* only a *few* of the *thousands* of *adversities* which actually *could* happen to you—and you feature *them* in your mental HORROR MOVIE, re-run over . . . and over . . . and over . . . again!

If you think back over your life, you will find some interesting facts about the possible adversities which *you selected to worry about.*

(1) Most of the adversities which *you selected to worry about . . . never happened!*

(2) Most of the few adversities which *did* happen were *not nearly as disastrous* as you worried they might be. They probably did much less damage to you *than your worrying about them did!*

And, your worrying *did not prevent* their happening!

(3) Perhaps *several* of the adversities which you selected to worry about *did happen* as unpleasantly as you worried they would. *But you were obviously capable of handling them*—or you would not be able to read this book with *the expectation of succeeding in achieving your life-goal.*

And, your worrying could *not prevent* their happening!

Worrying never prevents anything from happening! You cannot worry your troubles away!

So . . . STOP the self-torture of constantly re-running the mental HORROR MOVIES of worry!

How?

Here's HELP! . . .

(*And this may surprise you!*)

(1)Turn back to the first chapter of this book.

(2) *Re-read every chapter*—hurriedly if you must, and thoroughly if you can—*but* give *every* chapter this *new title:* "HOW TO STOP WORRYING."

(3) You will find that *every chapter in this book* contains a practical lesson on HOW TO STOP WORRYING *which you can begin to use at once!*

(4) This book has many purposes: To enable

you to *achieve your life-goal* . . . to make you the *ideal person* you want to become . . . to goal-command your subconscious to guide you to, or attract to you, *whatever you want in life . . . happiness! . . . love! . . . success! . . . wealth! . . . influence! . . . power! . . . popularity! . . . fame!* . . . *WHATEVER you want!*

This book will condition your thinking so that you always will keep a QUIET MIND . . . *free from resentment . . . free from anger . . . free from all of the disturbing, destructive emotions.*

This book will teach you how to *succeed with people-problems,* how to *manage problem-people* (including *managing yourself,* if you are a problem-person).

And, this book will teach you *much, much more!*

While this book is teaching you all those things —there is *in every chapter* a practical, easy-to-use lesson on HOW TO STOP WORRYING! (It will not say so *in those exact words*—but the lesson is there!)

So . . . right now, review *every* chapter which you have read—and *discover for yourself* its lesson on HOW TO STOP WORRYING!

Chapter 29

Here's HELP!...

Put A PERIOD After It

It is an almost universal human failing that people either cannot or will not STOP what they should— when they should.

You could devote hours just to making a list of things which people persist in continuing long after they should have stopped. Thus they do themselves harm in varying degrees—from obesity continued to fatality, from anxiety continued to suicide.

The list could be endless and include almost everything. So we shall mention here only a few obvious examples.

People won't *stop* eating when they should *stop,* and thus they become satiated, grow fat and soon die.

People won't *stop* alcoholic drinking when they should *stop,* and so they become obnoxious drunks.

People won't *stop* talking when they should *stop,* and thus they become bores.

Those are just a few of countless PHYSICAL examples, chosen because they are so obvious, so frequent, and *so easily stopped*—as all PHYSICAL excesses can *so easily be stopped.*

Why can PHYSICAL excesses be *stopped so easily?*

It is because they are under the *direct control* of the *conscious mind*. You are *consciously* aware of them, or you could and should be. *So you can consciously stop by just consciously thinking:* "STOP!" And *mean* it!

And stopping any excess is no more difficult than that—*as long as it is entirely PHYSICAL and therefore controlled by the conscious mind and will.*

It is when excesses have an EMOTIONAL cause, which is in the *less controllable subconscious mind,* that stopping them becomes difficult. Even in the familiar examples just given, when they become *more emotional and less physical,* when they become *deeply subconscious instead of simply conscious,* the excesses become increasingly difficult to stop.

Let's review the preceding examples, now assuming that these excesses have EMOTIONAL causes:

Over-eating, too frequent eating, *can be compulsive*—a substitute, an over-compensation, an emotional relief. *The cause, then, is emotional and in the subconscious mind.* So it has to be treated as an *emotional* problem.

That also applies to excessive alcoholic drinking when it seeks escape from reality in distortion or numbness of feeling; in stupor or temporary oblivion. *Its cause is in the subconscious, and it is an emotional problem.*

And that applies to excessive talking which

overcompensates for an inferiority complex and is *emotionally compulsive*.

As soon as we start dealing with EMOTIONS, we have problems.

Since it is the purpose of this book to provide help in solving such problems . . . Here's HELP!

We started this chapter by saying that it is an almost universal human failing that people either cannot or will not stop what they should—when they should.

Then we pointed out that excesses with PHYSICAL causes are under direct control of the *conscious mind* and can be *stopped by conscious will*. So . . . no problem there. You just STOP.

But, excesses which have EMOTIONAL causes or are, themselves, emotions, have their causes in the *subconscious mind* and therefore are more difficult to stop. Stopping them requires HELP—which is what this book is about.

And what this chapter is about is WHEN to *stop* and HOW to *stop* when you are confronted with an *emotional* problem, because FAILURE TO STOP is one of the principal causes of trouble in this troubled world.

Here is a useful rule:

Never escalate a negative emotion.

Do not add emotional negatives. Let's apply this rule to the almost universal problem of criticism. Criticism seldom is worth its cost. It is best not to criticize at all. If you absolutely *must* criticize, *do no add emotion to criticism.* Do not *add* resentment, vindictiveness, irritation, hate or any *emotional negatives.* Criticize gently, inoffensively, with obvious goodwill, and with the disarming manner of suggesting a better method—and STOP right there. PUT A PERIOD AFTER IT. *Do not continue criticism until it becomes nagging.* PUT A PERIOD AFTER IT.

Most quarrels either start with, include, or escalate into, criticism. Decide, in advance, how far your criticism *must* go—then PUT A PERIOD AFTER IT. Do not *add* to your original criticism in the heat of a resulting argument. PERIOD. *Do not add emotion.* PUT A PERIOD AFTER IT. Do not argue the matter further. Do not discuss it further. *Never escalate a negative emotion.* PUT A PERIOD AFTER IT.

Take another example: *Hurt feelings.*

Your feelings have been hurt. Your ego (and everybody's ego) has *three indispensable desires:* (1) The desire to be *important.* (2) The desire to be *admired.* (3) The desire to be *appreciated.* Unfortunately, not all people know that. And some rude person has deflated your importance, or detracted from the admiration you justly deserve, or shown you no proper appreciation. So your feelings are hurt.

And you feel resentment. STOP right there. PUT A PERIOD AFTER IT. Ignore it. Forgive it. Forget it. But do not ADD to it! Because resentment escalates into dislike, and dislike escalates into hatred—just by your thinking about it! *Never escalate a negative emotion.* PUT A PERIOD AFTER IT. What has happened, has happened. PERIOD. You can't change the past. PERIOD. Do not dwell on it. PERIOD. Do not re-live it in your memory, over and over again. PUT A PERIOD AFTER IT. That's that. And that's all. PERIOD.

Or, perhaps you're worried. Most people are.

It is proper to be concerned if there is something you can do about it, but it is dangerous to be worried. Because, as in previous examples, EMOTIONAL ESCALATION takes hold and, unless you STOP it, worry escalates into anxiety, and anxiety escalates into fear, and fear escalates into . . . well, into things too horrible to describe here.

So if you're worried, convert your helpless worry into useful concern which thoughtfully and actively works to solve your problem. Whatever caused your worry, PUT A PERIOD AFTER IT. STOP right there! *Never escalate a negative emotion.* PERIOD. Do not *add* to it. PERIOD. Do not let it continue. PUT A PERIOD AFTER IT.

Or, you don't like somebody. (You don't *have* to like *everybody!*) But when you don't like somebody, PUT A PERIOD AFTER THEM. Be like late President Eisenhower who said, "I never waste a minute thinking about someone I don't like." He PUT A PERIOD AFTER THEM. And that's what you must do. So you don't like someone? Then . . . PERIOD. That's that. PERIOD. That's all. PERIOD. Give the matter no further thought. *Never escalate a negative emotion.* PUT A PERIOD AFTER IT.

Or, you have troubles? Who hasn't? Do not *add* to them by escalating them with grief or worry or fear. *Never escalate a negative emotion.* Deal with troubles as you can and if you must—but do not *add* to them. STOP right there. PUT A PERIOD AFTER THEM. Whatever has happened, has happened. PERIOD. "It is so, it cannot be otherwise." PERIOD.

When fate closes one door, faith always opens another. *You can depend on that.* PERIOD.

Chapter 30

Here's HELP! . . .

Are You Tortured By Your Clock?

Your clock should limit its place in your life to usefully telling you what time it is.

But do not let your clock become your *boss* and constantly *order* you to *hurry! . . . hurry! . . . hurry!*

And, especially, do not let your clock become an *instrument of torture* which applies *pressure! . . . and more pressure! . . . and more pressure!* Until you break.

Your clock can kill you!

Dr. Anthony Sidoni, Jr., Chief of Metabolics at the Philadelphia General Hospital said that if we leave some things to be done tomorrow, our chances of *living to do them* will increase materially.

But, you protest, there is so *much* to be done!

Sure there is!

But can you do it better from a hospital bed?

And a grave is even more confining.

You could seek help from the really expert

hurriers. They learned how to turn hurry into frustration . . . and frustration into worry . . . and *then rest*.

They are resting now . . . in the cemetery.

But they did not die in vain—if their early death from *hurry-frustration-worry* will teach us a lesson.

And the lesson is:

(1) If your clock is your boss . . .

(2) And then your clock becomes an instrument of torture which applies pressure . . . and more pressure . . . and more pressure . . .

(3) So that you hurry . . . hurry . . . hurry . . .

(4) Until you are frustrated, annoyed, irritated . . .

(5) And you worry . . . worry . . . worry . . .

(6) . . . . . . STOP!!!

It is better to STOP of your own volition—than to be stopped by death.

Because, if you STOP before death stops you, then you will still be alive—and can learn *the secret of the really big achievers*.

The really big achievers do not live by a clock —but by an hour-glass. They think of their tasks as grains of sand in an hour-glass . . . coming *one* at a time . . . *unhurried* . . . *one* at a time . . . *unhurried* . . . *one* at a time.

And they *complete each task* . . . *one* at a time . . . *unhurried* . . . *one* at a time . . . *unhurried* . . . *one* at a time.

The face of their clock *smiles* at them.

Does the face of *your* clock *smile* at YOU?

Chapter 31

Here's HELP! . . .

And Wise, Old Solomon Said ...

Some say that Solomon was the wisest of all men.

But what did Solomon say?

Solomon, whose name is symbolic of wisdom, said: "A soft answer turneth away wrath, but grievous words store up anger."

Then wise, old Solomon added: "He that is slow to wrath is of great understanding, but he that is hasty of spirit exalteth folly."

Well?

YOU can do those four simple things can't you? (1) Always give a soft answer. (2) Never speak irritating words. (3) Do not over-react in anger. (4) Do not act rashly.

Thus, advised Solomon, one of the wisest men of all time. Four *easy* things which you can *easily* do—and which can *easily* change your life! *Think about it.*

Chapter 32

Here's HELP! . . .

Do Not OVER-React To Trouble Which Has Not Even Happened!

It is one of the lessons of this book to teach its readers not to OVER-react to emotionally disturbing situations—*when such events happen.*

It is worth a brief chapter to point out that while emotionally OVER-reacting to past and present situations is seriously self-damaging—emotionally OVER-reacting to something *which has not even happened* is just plain ridiculous!

Like the children who got into a big argument over where to bury the family's pet bird.

One child argued that the pet bird deserved an honored burial in the front yard.

Another child argued (even more loudly) that the pet bird should be buried in a more secluded place in the back yard.

Then another child argued (much more

loudly) that the family's pet bird should be buried in the country on a wooded hillside.

By the time the argument reached the yelling stage, the mother pointed out that the bird wasn't *dead* yet!

And, in fact, the family didn't even *have* a pet bird!

They had merely *talked* about buying a pet bird *sometime in the future*. Maybe.

Many people are like those children. They *imagine* all sorts of future tragedies, disasters, troubles. Then they OVER-react *emotionally* to events which *haven't even happened!*

It simply is ridiculous to become *upset emotionally* about *imagined* troubles which *haven't even happened*—and perhaps never will.

It is worse than ridiculous; *it is dangerous!*

You cannot live in the future—today.

You can only live in the present—today.

To add the *imagined* burdens of *tomorrow* to the real burdens of today will *double* your load.

Then to further add *imagined* burdens of *future weeks and months*—*will overwhelm you.*

"Sufficient unto *each* day . . ."

Chapter 33

Here's HELP! . . .

Get A Rescue Boat

The preceding chapter warned against *emotionally RE-acting* to imagined trouble which *has not even happened.*

But this does not mean that you should neglect being mentally, emotionally and spiritually *prepared* to cope with *whatever* troubles may come.

You should not *imagine* all sorts of *possible* troubles and *emotionally* OVER-react to them.

You should not *emotionally* OVER-react *at all!*

But you should *prudently prepare* so that you will not be overwhelmed by events which may rush upon you like a flood of troubled waters.

Troubled waters!

We build our personal dike against time. But, sometimes the volume of trouble is too much for our man-made bulwark and, under pressure, our dike begins to leak.

Like the little Dutch boy, we bravely thrust

our hand into the first break to stop the flow. But there's a persistence about troubled waters, like the much-quoted "tide in the affairs of men".

If we haven't our dike of resistence high enough and strong enough, the rising waters of trouble will crush it or overflow it.

Then we shall be submerged in our seas of troubles and drowned in calamity. Unless we have provided for such an emergency . . . *and have a rescue boat.*

When we seek protection against a floodtide of troubles, a boat is better than dike. A dike is useful, but limited.

The function of a dike is to resist. We should plan and build our means of resisting the regular flow of troubles which are a natural part of life. Otherwise every trouble trickle will be unimpeded and we shall be too much occupied in dealing with the trivial.

The human nervous system has what psychiatrists call an "emotional threshold". Over this threshold pour the fears, anxieties, hatreds, resentments and the whole flood of emotions—directly into our consciousness.

By raising the height of our emotional threshold—by increasing the height of our dike against trouble—we block the lesser of these trouble-emotions so that they never reach our consciousness at all. Otherwise we would be plagued by an *over-sensitivity to emotions* and become distraught even to insanity.

So a dike has an important place in our managing reasonably the normal ebb and flow of troubles.

How do we build this dike which raises our threshold against unwanted emotional feelings? The means are many and most are described individually in separate chapters in this book, so we shall not repeat them here.

Besides, this chapter is about *a rescue boat to keep you safely afloat when troubles reach a floodtide* which pours in torrents over the dike of your normal resistance.

The value of a *boat* is that it will keep you *on top* of trouble, no matter how *deep* its swirling waters.

Your rescue boat assures the confidence that *you can ride out any flood of troubles* by remaining serenely *on top,* and that the depth of your troubles is of no consequence to your boat because it will continue to float *on top* of *any* depth.

It is well—and it may be *essential*—to have such an imaginary boat *always ready in your mind* for emergency rescue in times of deep trouble.

And, it is appropriate that such a boat should have a name which properly describes it.

The name of my *emergency rescue boat is* "FAITH".

What's the name of *your* rescue boat?

Chapter 34

Here's HELP!...

Proven Success Method: Less Criticizing And More Sympathizing

Do you want to be popular? Try *less criticizing* and *more sympathizing!*

Do you want to be loved? Try *less criticizing* and *more sympathizing!*

Do you want to influence people? Try *less criticizing* and *more sympathizing!*

Do you want to succeed? Try *less criticizing* and *more sympathizing!*

Criticizing turns people OFF!

Sympathizing turns people ON!

It is just as simple as *that!*

Having stated it simply, let us now examine the facts, the reasons which prove the foregoing statements.

(1) *To be popular,* be less criticizing and more sympathizing:

Criticism is the cause of many (perhaps most)

of our unpleasant and unsatisfactory relationships with others.

Criticism is an open attack on another person's precious ego (self). Even if your criticism is "justified", it still hurts the other emotionally and incurs resentment instantly and, often, hatred and lasting hostility.

Criticism is deeply implanted in the other's subconscious which feeds it into his or her conscious thought often whenever the criticizer is seen or even mentioned.

Criticism is *no* way to make or keep friends.

Sympathizing *is!*

And I do not mean sympathy only in terms of consoling grief.

Sympathizing combines understanding, agreement and *emotional acceptance.* It is not limited, but is an all-encompassing togetherness.

As Sir Thomas Talfourd taught, "Sympathy is the *first* great lesson which man should learn." And not only learn—but frequently *express* through understanding, agreement and emotional acceptance.

Without sympathy (*understanding, agreement* and *emotional acceptance*), friendship is reduced to mere acquaintanceship.

(2) *To be loved,* do less criticizing and more sympathizing:

Edmund Burke, the great English orator and statesman, proclaimed, "Next to love, sympathy is the divinest passion of the human heart."

With love being the *most* divine passion of the human heart, and sympathy being the *next most* divine passion, then *frequently expressed love and sympathy* (*understanding, agreement* and *emotional acceptance*) are the *essentials* of enduring love.

When sympathy is *used* in its total meaning of "understanding, agreement and emotional acceptance"— you can see *how vital is sympathy to love and marriage.*

Many divorces are the result of the belief (openly expressed, or suppressed in the subconscious) that "He (or she) doesn't *understand* me!" Which, in psychology, means: "He (or she) doesn't understand me because he (or she) *doesn't sympathize with my problems, feelings, etc.,* and, therefore, does not *really love* me."

Before marriage, couples should test their *enduring compatibility* in terms of this wise statemnet by Sir Richard Steele:

"There is a kind of sympathy in souls that fits them for each other; and we may be assured when we see two persons engaged in the warmths of mutual affection, that there are certain qualities in both their minds which bear a resemblance to one another."

(3) *To influence people,* do less criticizing and more sympathizing:

You cannot influence others if you do not frequently express your sympathy (*understanding, agreement* and *emotional acceptance*) for *their* cause, *their* beliefs, *their* hopes, *their* ideals.

To attempt to influence others from an adverse and opposite position—*to be unsympathetic with the people and thoughts* which you are trying to influence—is as stupid as it is ineffective.

You cannot influence others if you try to en-

force your own unsympathetic point-of-view upon them, but only if you *"put yourself in their place"*, *understand* and *sympathize* with their *point-of-view,* and submit your proposal in terms of *their* objectives as a means of *helping them* get what *they* want.

(4) *To succeed,* do less criticizing and more sympathizing.

No longer can ruthless men succeed, in any meaningful and permanent way, by climbing to success over the struggling bodies of their fellow workers.

You must be *lifted* to success *by your fellow men.*

The secret: *Make yourself easy to lift!*

You do *not* inspire others to lift you to success by *criticizing* them.

But when others are convinced that you are *sympathetic to their goals,* they gladly will help you attain a higher position because by doing so they are putting you in a better position to help them attain *their goals,* too.

Bernard Baruch used to say, "Two things are bad for the heart: *Running up stairs* and *running down people.*"

By not running down people (criticizing them), you will find them more willing to help you upstairs (to success).

It will be good for your heart.
Physically . . . and spiritually.

Chapter 35

Here's HELP! ...

Let The EXPERTS Do It

The world is full of *do-it-yourself* people.

Many are self-proclaimed authorities on subjects concerning which they have only limited knowledge.

Others are self-appointed experts in activities for which they have inadequate training and little skill.

Being a do-it-yourself person is commendable in the pursuit of avocations and hobbies—or these would provide no pleasure and no pride of accomplishment.

Being a do-it-yourself person is desirable when that is the simplest, quickest way to do the innumerable *ordinary* tasks of our lives—provided that the results are acceptable and the damage resulting from inexperience and lack of skill is minimal.

But when the task requires *specialized knowledge, technical training, exceptional skills, professional abilities,* which you do not have—LET THE EXPERTS DO IT.

Certainly, there are many such specialized tasks for which the knowledge and skill requirements are so formidable that no novice would attempt them; so we need not consider them here.

It is the border-line cases that get us into trouble:

When we are so sure of our own knowledge of the law that we involve ourselves legally without benefit of the advice of an attorney; when we indulge unwisely in the ever-present opportunities for self-medication; when, unaided by expert accountants, we prepare complicated tax returns and financial documents; when, with too-little knowledge and skill, we become plumbers, electricians, mechanics, real estate buyers or sellers, carpenters, investors, designers, decorators, and . . . well, you name it, and too many people will try to do it, without adequate knowledge and training, and with results which range from amusing to pathetic to tragic.

The self-satisfaction and the admiration of others which result from accomplishments outside your known qualifications, are admittedly tempting.

But the risks involved are usually unsuspected. And therein lies the danger. The danger often is considerable—and it may be catastrophic.

With exceptions, too few to consider, *there simply are NO tasks that require the knowledge and skill of experts which can be done as well, if at all, by novices.*

If the task, even possibly, may require the knowledge and skill of an expert, you will save time, money, trouble and worry if you LET THE EXPERT DO IT.

It has been my experience, in a rather long and

very eventful life, that *the services of highly qualified experts in all specialized endeavors always are worth more than they cost.* I am by no means alone in that opinion. I think you will find agreement among all widely experienced businessmen and all knowledgeable people.

If you start now, and make it a rule for the rest of your life, to LET THE EXPERTS DO IT, *your savings in time, money, trouble and worry will be enormous!*

And letting the experts do it, not only will *save* you money, it will *make* you money. *No sizable fortune ever has been amassed* (except rarely by luck) *without the help of some experts and usually many experts.*

An important part of the technique of LETTING THE EXPERTS DO IT, is to *let* them. Which means do not employ an expert and then waste his time with your novice suggestions and advice. When an expert wants information from you, he will ask for it. When an expert wants advice, he will ask *another expert—not you.* The expert may ask for your opinion as a guide to *what* you want, but if he asks your advice on *how* to do it, he is no expert, but just a con man, whom you should promptly replace with a genuine expert.

One of the important advantages of LETTING THE EXPERTS DO IT, is that it relieves you of worry about how the tasks will be done and the final outcome. So, having thus relieved yourself of worry—*do not worry.* If worrying is involved, that is part of the expert's job; that is part of what you are paying for, and in no event should you take over any part of the worrying.

Remember the advice of psychologist-philosopher, William James, "When once a decision has been reached and execution is the order of the day, dismiss absolutely all responsibility and care (anxiety) for the outcome." Do not reconsider. Do not doubt. Have absolute confidence in your expert. Express your confidence to him. If any worrying is to be done, let the expert worry. After all, you're paying him for it. Just relax and let the expert do the job—in his own expert way.

This chapter on LET THE EXPERTS DO IT would be incomplete without recommending the always-available assistance of *THE Expert. No matter how many mortal experts you assign to your tasks, you need the Master Expert as Overseer.*

For the *Master Expert,* no task is too small, such as arranging the microcosm of atoms; no task is too big, such as operating with absolute precision an infinite universe of trillions of whirling planetary systems through limitless space throughout an eternity which had no beginning and can have no end.

That is the kind of Master Expert, who should be in charge of your life. He is as near as your thoughts— and available through your subconscious as described in this book.

So . . . LET THE EXPERTS DO IT—*and let the Master Expert boss the job.*

Chapter 36

Here's HELP! . . .

Patience Power

Of all people, a Norman crusader, with flashing sword and with banner unfurled, would seem to be the least likely to teach the power of patience.

Yet, that is what happened. The stalwart Norman crusader, Tancred, declared, *"Everything comes if a man will only wait."*

That is a lesson which has had to be taught and re-taught by history—throughout history: the quiet, calm, sure power of patience. *It has had to be taught again and again because people persist in associating power with action—instant, compulsive action . . . NOW!*

Since those who will not learn from history are doomed to repeat its mistakes, then, obviously, someone is going to have to teach the *power of patience* to our restless, heedless "NOW Generation" so let us first lay the foundation with the granite of history's solid wisdom which has withstood both trivia and time.

J. G. Holland, the American author, was not content to "only wait", but added the obvious advantage of working while waiting: *"There is no great achievement that is not the result of working and waiting."*

"Patience Power" is not just a slogan to be brushed lightly aside. Joseph De Maistre, the French writer (1754–1821) insisted, *"To know how to wait is the great secret of success."* And, that's about as unequivocally as it can be stated.

Being a clergyman, Horace Bushnell, said it more gently, but none the less positively, a century ago: *"It is not necessary for all men to be great in action. The greatest and sublimest power is often simple patience."*

And, from that most quotable of all writers, Shakespeare: *"How poor are they who have not patience! What wound did ever heal but by degrees?"* How better can we identify patience with Nature? Think of Nature's healing of a wound. Always gradually . . . patiently. *The deeper the wound, the slower the healing—and the more patience required.* It is a *Law of Nature,* which those who would inflict deep emotional wounds, and those who suffer them, should ponder . . . and each learn *"Patience Power".*

Did you ever engage in the rewarding pleasure of making thought-chains? Let's start with the subject of this chapter: *"Patience Power"*, and link together the thoughts of different people—starting with Tyron Edwards, the American author of the past century. He wrote, *"He that is patient will persevere."*

"Patient perseverance" links, in our thought-chain to "persistence", such as described by President Calvin Coolidge: *"Nothing will take the place of patient per-*

sistence. *Talent will not. Nothing is more commonplace than unsuccessful men with talent. Genius will not: unrewarded genius is almost a proverb. Education will not; the world is full of educated derelicts. Persistence (patient perseverance) and determination alone are omnipotent."*

We link our thought-chain to Samuel Smiles' wise observation: *"To determine upon attainment is frequently attainment itself; earnest resolution has often seemed to have about it almost a savor of omnipotence."*

This not only is an example of making thought-chains, but also a demonstration of how each thought-link, while related to it, is one more step away from our original subject—which we remind ourselves is *"Patience Power"*, about which the French poet, Jean La Fontaine wrote, *"Patience and time do more than strength and passion."* To which we must add a related admonition from John Dryden, *"Beware of the fury of a patient man."*

As we learned in our thought-chain, *patience is linked with perseverance.* The French naturalist, Georges Louis Buffon, put it this way, *"Hold on; hold fast; hold out. Patience is genius."* And the American theologian, Nathaniel Emmons, emphasized the power of patient perseverance, *"Steady, patient, persevering thinking will generally surmount every obstacle in the search for truth."*

There is this continued linking of *patience with perseverance* in order to attain success and greatness, in the teachings of Jean de la Bruyere, the French essayist, *"There is no road too long to the man who advances deliberately and without haste; no honors too distant to the man who prepares himself for them with patience."*

But, as we have learned, patience must be

linked with perseverance, because, as Napoleon said, *"Victory belongs to the persevering."*

It is worth noting that this powerful, ruthless, military conqueror should single out the quality of *perseverance* as the means of victory.

Yet, it is so. And those of us with ordinary talent can depend on the positive assurance of the great and wise English philanthropist, Sir Thomas Fowell Buxton: *"With ordinary talent and extraordinary perseverance, all things are obtainable."*

So what is it *you* want to obtain?

Sir Buxton said you can get it through extraordinary *perseverance*.

And wise, old Ben Franklin called it *patience* when he wrote: *"He that can have patience can have what he will."*

Let us call it both:

Patient perseverance!

With patient perseverance *"all things are obtainable"* and *"you can have what you will"*.

Chapter 37

Here's HELP! ...

The Lesson Of The Birds

When man gets ready to fly—in his prop plane, his jet plane, his mighty missile, he prudently *waits* for the lift required to become airborne. Unless ample power is provided—*in advance*—man will not make the attempt to fly. And wisely so.

I do not criticize man's prudence in this mode of transportation which requires his dependence on mechanical means. I simply want to contrast man's flying with that of the birds.

While man properly waits for enough power *in advance* of take-off or lift-off, the bird *confidently pushes off from its perch,* simultaneously waves its wings and easily flies—*without fear that the power for flying will not be provided AS NEEDED.*

We will concede that the bird is better equipped for flying on two counts: (1) The bird was designed by nature to fly, and: (2) The bird has an inner sense which assures it that the power to fly will be provided *any time it pushes off from its perch*—that BY DOING, IT WILL RECEIVE THE POWER.

And that is our lesson from the birds, not to be able to fly as they do, which obviously we cannot, but to acquire the unquestioning FAITH that BY DOING, WE WILL RECEIVE THE POWER—*not to fly, but to surmount, in our human way, the obstacles of life.*

Imagine a bird, perched on a limb, frantically flapping its wings *waiting* to be lifted! Yet that is what man does when he frantically *waits* for enough power—*in advance*—before pushing off into his human environment *to achieve what he really could*, if he only realized that BY DOING, HE WOULD RECEIVE THE POWER.

If we *wait* to be lifted to the heights of personal achievement, if we make no attempt until we are assured of the necessary power *in advance*, we shall remain, flapping frantically on our present perch, clutching to it with indecision, hesitation and fear—until time breaks us lose and we fall down . . . down . . .

Every time we see a bluebird fly or an eagle soar, it should remind us that only BY DOING, WE RECEIVE THE POWER TO DO. *We should learn that the personal power to achieve comes with the DOING and is not provided wholly in advance of the effort.*

Thus, the more we DO, the more power we receive for DOING, *and our own action becomes the generator of greater action!*

But how do we differentiate between prudence and fear? How do we know IF we should make the attempt? When should we push off from our safe perch toward greater heights of personal achievement?

There is a *Law of Life* which states: *"Whatever man can conceive and BELIEVE, man can achieve."*

To that eternal law, we can add the lesson of the birds: BY DOING, WE WILL RECEIVE THE POWER.

How can this be possible, that by the *act* of DOING, we generate or receive the *power* to DO?

One answer comes from the psychologists.

The most conservative psychologists say that a person seldom uses more than *half* of his actual capability. So simply by DOING, you will *double* your power!

Many psychologists say that a person operates only at one-tenth capacity. They say you are capable of doing *ten times* as much! Simply by DOING!

So you have from *twice* to *ten times* more power than you are using. Therefore you can DO from *twice* to *ten times* as much—just by DOING it!

But there is much more power available to you than that. There is *Infinite Power* which provides the power to the entire universe and everything in it—*including you!*

So there is as much power available as you have *faith* to use.

If a little bird can have the *faith* to reach to its destination—surely *you* can have *faith* that will supply you the kind and amount of power to reach *your goal.*

AS YOU DO . . . YOU WILL RECEIVE!

Chapter 38

Here's HELP! . . .

What Kind Of Impression Do
You REALLY Make On Others?

One of our greatest handicaps in self-improvement is that we do not know—*or we judge incorrectly*—the kind of impression *we really make on others.*

We need to see ourselves—*through the critical eyes of others.*

We need to hear our voices—both our manner of speaking (voice tone, sincerity, enthusiasm, etc.) and the correctness with which we use the language—*through the critical ears of others.*

We need to examine our total personality—through knowing the personal effect (magnetism, repulsiveness, or whatever degree in between)—*through the critical evaluation of others as they judge our personality.*

We need to know the effect of *what* we are saying—*by examining whether it is welcomed, accepted or rejected by the minds of others.*

And these are but a few of the things we need to know *from the point of view of others*—if we are to achieve any meaningful self-improvement.

You do not live *alone* in this world—but live in a world increasingly crowded with *other people*.

These *other people* in your world can make or break you. *And eventually they will do one or the other!*

Depending upon the impression you make on them.

It will do you no good to lull yourself into a *false* sense of security by reading in the poem: "I am the *master* of my fate" unless you realize that you will "*master your fate*" only to the extent that you *master proven success methods* and *constantly use* them to make a favorable impression on *others* and to successfully influence *others*.

As this book and all of my books emphasize: *you positively cannot achieve great success, or even mediocre success, without the goodwill and cooperation of other people*—usually *many* other people.

You cannot *climb* to success *over* others; you must be *lifted* to success *by* them.

People will not *lift you to success* unless you have made a *favorable impression on them* and *successfully influence them to want to help you*.

Since, like all human beings, you are *not naturally endowed* with either the knowledge or ability to achieve the degree of favorable impression and successful influence necessary *to motivate others to lift you to success* —these self-improvement and success methods must be *learned, perfected,* and *constantly used*.

The proven success methods, which I have

researched over a period of forty years, are available to you in this book and in my other books, so this chapter will not attempt to discuss any success method—*but one.*

And *this* may be the most important success method of all! It is the need, as described throughout this chapter, for you to learn and constantly use self-improvement and proven success methods *as they relate to others* —to favorably impress *others;* to successfully influence *others.*

Accomplishment for SELF-satisfaction may bring you limited *selfish* pleasure—but you must gear your achievements to OTHERS-satisfaction if you expect *those others to lift you to success.*

There is a current trend toward SELF-gratification in everything from clothing and manners to insolent disregard for the ultimately necessary approval of others.

This "others-be-damned" attitude is not the way to be lifted to success by those same "others".

Those "same others", or their friends or their friends's friends, have a way of appearing unexpectedly in *career-deciding* situations. You will regret it if you ever have demonstrated your "self-expression" (really "selfish-expression") in disregard for their necessary approval.

It is better—*it is necessary*—to focus your self-improvement and success methods on *favorably impressing and successfully influencing others to WANT to lift you to success.*

Before you *say* or *do* anything—ask yourself the crucial question:

"Will this make me EASIER TO LIFT?"

Chapter 39

Here's HELP! . . .

And Then Ask:
"Compared To WHAT?"

It is well known that the always-questioning Greek philosopher, Socrates, was married to nagging shrew who devoted her life to trying to make the philosopher miserable.

One day a friend asked Socrates how his wife was. Typically, Socrates replied with a question.

Socrates asked, "Compared to WHAT?"

Like all of Socrates' questions, there is great wisdom hidden in the inquiry, "Compared to WHAT?"

People, places, situations, events—yes, and emotional feelings—are relative. *They are good or bad in degree—depending upon with what they are compared.*

This fact of life furnishes us a very useful technique for dealing with the people, places, situations and events in our daily lives—and our mental-emotional reaction to them.

The question, "Compared to WHAT?", will teach us tolerance and moderation. It will teach us not to OVER-react, but in the words of Kipling: "Meet with triumph and disaster; and treat those two imposters just the same."

The question: "Compared to WHAT?" will teach us not to seek halos for little generosities; not to make triumphs out of modest accomplishments; not to make disasters out of minor disappointments.

For all these things are *relative,* and are put in their proper places by the simple question: "Compared to WHAT?" A few brief examples:

(1) *People:* There are as many kinds of people as there are people. So when we OVER-react to some person as being offensive and intolerable, we should ask: "Compared to WHAT?" By *comparison,* the objectionable person is *relatively* less offensive and intolerable than many situations, events, and other people. And we become more tolerant.

The black youth who cuts classes in school, refuses educational opportunities, won't take a job, gets into all kinds of miscellaneous mischief—then struts around with an extreme Afro hair-do and weird clothes, loudly proclaiming that *he* is an exhibit of *black pride* . . . should ask himself: "Compared to WHAT (or more grammatically, to WHOM)?" To Dr. Charles Drew, the distinguished Negro doctor who developed the means of preserving blood plasma and saved millions of lives of *all* races?

(2) *Places:* People who devote their great wealth to building mansions on expensively landscaped

estates, and proudly think: "Look, what I have built!" should ask: "Compared to WHAT?" Then, they should look at a picture of what Dr. Albert Schweitzer built—a primitive "hospital" in steaming tropical Africa, where amid pythons, gorillas, and wild savages, he treated the sick natives of another race.

Or, the people who build "castles" to house their "valuable" worldly possessions, and smirk: "Look what I have built?" should ask: "Compared to WHAT?" and look at what Sir Christopher Wren built—the magnificent St. Paul's Cathedral in London—to house eternal "possessions".

(3) *Situations and Events:* Whatever happens to affect our lives is *relative* to past, present, or *possible* events. We put events into perspective by asking: "Compared to WHAT?" There have been, are now, and undoubtedly will be, better and worse events. Each event, good or bad, always has passed—always will—with the ticking of the clock and the changing of the calendar. Even while it lasts, each situation is not the ultimate ecstasy or tragedy—but only relative: "Compared to WHAT?"

(4) *Emotions:* We must remember that it is not *what* happens, but how we *feel* about it, that really matters. Before we OVER-react emotionally, let us calmly appraise the impact of each incident "Compared to WHAT?" Judged, unemotionally, in comparative relativity, we will find that the incident deserves not our OVER-reaction but our shrugging off as one of life's incessant trivialities. This is a way to moderation and tolerance.

Compared to WHAT?

Chapter 40

Here's HELP! . . .

Some Things You Should "NO!"

This is not a chapter about morals.

It is assumed that you have the morality and good sense to say a firm, clear "NO!" to what is *wrong*.

But this chapter recommends that you say "NO!" to what is *right*.

There are literally millions of things in this world which *are right* and which *need to be done*—but to which you must mentally, if not vocally, say: "NO!"

No one person has the time and the ability to do any but a few things which need to be done.

So the *proven success method* is this:

(1) Say "NO!" generally.

(2) Say "YES!" *very, very selectively*.

Let's take a closer look:

(1) Say "NO!" *generally:* You simply *must concentrate* your thought, time and effort on your *one main goal*.

You cannot possibly do all of the things you will be *asked* to do. And the more successful and famous you become, the more things you will be asked to do. Often you will be offered large sums of money or other benefits. Often you will be asked to donate your proven ability to helping worthy charitable causes, and they will tug at your heart.

But remember the rule:

(1) Say "NO!" *generally.*

(2) Say "YES!" *very, very selectively.*

Let us refer again to the teaching of William James, famed psychologist of Harvard University. He taught that *"belief creates the actual fact"* provided that you *concentrate* on achieving what you want *"exclusively and do not wish at the same time a hundred other incompatible things just as strongly."*

So you are going to have to say "NO!" to a lot of desirable and worthwhile things, simply because they are *"incompatible"* with the necessary work you *must* do to reach *your main goal.*

William James taught you must concentrate *"exclusively"* on *your main goal.*

So you must say "NO!" *generally.*

This has been taught by all of the wisest of great thinkers. Perhaps it was said best by the eloquent English statesman, William Gladstone:

"To comprehend a man's life, it is necessary to know not merely what he *does,* but what he *purposely leaves undone.*

"There is a *limit* that can be got out of a human body or a human brain, and he is a wise man who wastes no

142

time on pursuits for which he is not fitted; and he is still wiser, who, from the things he can do well, *chooses and resolutely follows the best.*"

So said one of the greatest of all statesmen. To re-state it less eloquently, but more concisely:

(1) Say "NO!" *generally.*

(2) Say "YES!" *very, very selectively.*

Remember that *your goal-reaching* servo-mechanism is your *subconscious,* and your subconscious functions in much the same way as an electronic, computerized guidance system. Direct it with *one exclusive goal-command* and your subconscious will guide you to, or attract to you, *the means and the power to achieve your life-goal.*

But if you direct your subconscious guidance-system to guide you to *many different goals* in *many different directions*—the resulting "*cross-circuits*" will "*blow a fuse.*" And you will have *no power* to reach *any* goal!

So you must say "NO!" *generally*—to everything which would be a significant *distraction* from your *concentrated thought and effort to reach your main goal.*

And you must say "YES!" *very, very selectively* —only to the offers and requests which are *compatible* with *your main goal.*

By saying "NO!" to many things, desirable but irrelevant, you clear the "YES!" road directly to your goal in life.

And you cannot achieve it otherwise.

Chapter 41

Here's HELP! . . .

Do NOT "Do It NOW!"

With all the instant activists rushing about, putting up little reminder signs urging us to "Do It NOW!" . . . it may be prudent for us to sit back, relax, and consider the wise advice of those who caution: "Do NOT Do It NOW!"

Beginning with God, who commanded, "Be *still* . . . and know that I am God." We can find God everywhere, because He *is* everywhere—but it is when *we are still* that we communicate most easily with God. Learn the art of *being still* . . . and listening.

As poet Bryan Waller Procter wrote, "*The mightest powers by deepest calms are fed.*" And so they are. Learn the QUIET MIND method taught earlier in this book—so that you can achieve the *deep calm* necessary for *mighty power.*

Tyron Edwards said it this way: "There are many times and circumstances in life when *our strength is to sit still.*"

144

There is an art of delay. It is the art of *"Doing nothing with a great deal of skill,"* as Cowper described it.

This does not advocate laziness, because it may require more effort to *restrain our eagerness* than to act instantly—*and rashly.* Certainly, it requires more judgment.

As Charles Simmons wrote, *"He who takes time to think and consider will act more wisely than he who acts hastily and on impulse."*

It is wise to keep a problem in suspense, without prejudice, until you arrive at a clear, satisfactory solution.

Problem solving requires not instant action, not eagerly grasping the *first* possible solution—but the quiet, calm evaluation of *all available alternatives.*

And, until you have thoughtfully considered *all available alternatives* and satisfied your own judgment concerning the *right* action to take—simply maintain what the American statesman, John Randolph, described as: *"Thoughtful, disciplined, intended inaction."*

Or what another great American statesman, John C. Calhoun, described as: *"Masterly inactivity."* Do not rush rashly!

There is a wise, old proverb: "If your tree bears fruit, rejoice—*but do not pick it until it is ripe."*

Remember the old story of Johnny Appleseed? Wherever he went, he planted apple seeds.

You be like that—*only you plant success seeds!* Plant the seeds *for your future success* constantly, wherever you go, whatever you do.

Then you will have an abundant harvest of

success—*to enjoy when you have allowed it time to ripen to perfection.*

Of course, succeed as fast as you can—but *do not try to succeed faster than you can!*

People who try to succeed *faster than they can* —get into trouble.

It is easier to *stay* out of trouble—than to *get* out of it.

Use *"thoughtful, disciplined, intended inaction"'* until you have calmly considered *all available alternatives* and satisfied your own judgment concerning the *right* action to take.

It is better to "Do It RIGHT" than to "Do It NOW".

Never break open an egg to get a baby chick out.

Chapter 42

Here's HELP! . . .

How To Live To Be 100

This chapter is not about just staying alive—but *staying healthy, active, mentally alert and happy for 100 years.*

I cannot guarantee it. Nobody can guarantee that you will live one more minute.

But I can tell you *how a large number of people actually do live to be 100* and, often, years longer than that.

There are various areas in the world where a much higher than average percentage of the population continues to be healthy, even vigorous, after they have past their hundredth birthday. They are mentally alert and their memories are clear and accurate.

Why?

(1) The people who are most likely to live more than 100 years *eat fewer calories*. The daily calorie consumption varies in each group but ranges from 1,200

to 1,900 calories per day. Compare this with the average calorie consumption in the United States of 3,300 calories per day. Of course, none of the 100-and-over group is fat or even over-weight. But neither are they under-nourished, as can be seen by their appearance, health, vigor and stamina.

(2) The 100-and-over people *eat more protein* and *much less animal fat,* and *very much less cholesterol* than those who die at earlier ages.

(3) The 100-and-over people get plenty of healthful *exercise every day.*

(4) The 100-and-over people *EXPECT to live to be over 100.*

They have a "youthful attitude" toward life. They feel "young" at *seventy* and happily say so. And they *simply take it for granted* that they will live more than a hundred years. *They consider 100 or more years to be their normal, natural life expectancy.*

I have no personal expertise in the field of gerontology; I am simply reporting some of the scientific facts concerning aging. You can reach your own conclusions concerning diet and exercise.

But there is one conclusion which applies to all of us in our daily activities and, especially, in our seeking to achieve our life-goals.

That is the *Law of Expectancy.* You will note that the people who live to be over 100, EXPECT to live to be over 100.

It is interesting that the *Law of Expectancy* seems to apply, not only to daily living, *but even to the length of life, itself.* Of course, there are other factors. But it is known that people *who expect to die soon, usually do.* And, people who *intensely want to die soon* (for a variety of reasons, often psychotic) *usually do die soon.*

What a powerful combination—or call it "sequence"—are (1) DESIRE, (2) BELIEF, (3) EXPECTANCY! *They influence, to a proven extent, even the power of life and death!*

But let us leave those two imponderables of life and death to a Greater Power.

Let us concentrate on applying the *"magic three" Laws of Life:* (1) the *Law of Desire,* (2) the *Law of Believing* and (3) the *Law of Expectancy* to achieving our life-goals.

These three *Laws of Life* are known as the *"magic three"* because they work like magic in producing in our lives *whatever we want* as our life-goal!

Here's HOW to use them:

(1) You must *intensely desire* your life-goal;

(2) You must *deeply believe* that you will attain your life-goal;

(3) You must *confidently expect* that you will surely achieve it.

These *"magic three" Laws of Life* are mentioned in this chapter because, along with many other factors, they even seem to *influence* the *length* of our lives.

But what is more important, these *"magic three" Laws of Life* actually *establish the quality of our lives* and *enable us to reach our life-goals* . . . as taught in other chapters of this book.

Chapter 43

Here's HELP! . . .

This 3-G Method Will Make You Popular, Successful And Happy

If you want to be *popular,* you must be popular with *people.* That's what popularity is all about.

If you want to be *successful,* you must be successful with *people.* Even if you were a lone prospector and discovered gold, your success still would depend upon the value that *people* would set on your gold and the willingness of *people* to buy it.

In business and in all endeavors, your *success* depends upon the response of *people.* The ultimate achievement is to get *other people to lift you to success.* To do this you must make yourself *"easy to lift",* which means that you must cause other people to *want* to lift *you* to success.

If you want to be happy, you must be happy *with people.* Solitary happiness is shallow and not fully satisfying. Ask those who have tried it!

The only deeply satisfying happiness is in the companionship and love of *people*.

So, what this chapter really is about, is how to be *popular, successful* and *happy*—with *people*.

The author has devised a very simple, easy and proven method for you to use to achieve this very desirable and deeply satisfying goal.

I call it the 3-G Method because it requires that you always do three things which have the initial letter "G."

This is the 3-G Method:

You *always*—without exception—*must do the following three things* whenever you are with any person or persons for as long as several minutes; or whenever you talk for as long as several minutes over the telephone; or whenever you write a note or letter:

(1G) *Always express GRATITUDE.* This is easy. With constant use, it will become automatic. You always can think of *something* for which to *express gratitude*, even if it is only for the other person's taking time to talk with you or read your letter, or consider your request or whatever. Hopefully, in most cases, you will be able to think of something more impressive and more memorable, because it is valuable to be *remembered* as a person who *always expresses gratitude*.

People want (*subconsciously need*) to be appreciated. When you *express gratitude*, you fulfill their subconscious need to be appreciated. So it is much more than just a friendly amenity. It has a deep, lasting effect.

(2G) *Always express GOODWILL.* Do not assume that your friends or even your family take your goodwill for granted. They want to *hear it expressed*. And, of course, they want to *see frequent, tangible evidences* of your goodwill in your relations with them. But demonstrating goodwill, as important as that is, is not enough. You also must *express* goodwill on every possible occasion.

Always sincerely expressing your goodwill to *everyone* you meet, phone or write will work miracles in your life!

(3G) *Always express GOOD WISHES!* Do not assume that everyone—*or anyone*—you meet, phone or write is aware of and favorably impressed by the fact that you specifically, consciously and earnestly wish them well.

In fact, if you do not actually *express* your *good wishes,* people will unconsciously assume that you do not particularly care. And they will consciously or subconsciously *feel indifferent toward you!*

Not only is it extremely important to enthusiastically *express* your *good wishes* and *goodwill* to everybody—but you can virtually produce "miracles" by *mentally broadcasting* your good wishes and goodwill even to people you do not know but would like to include in your *"personality radiation".* Anybody can do it and it is fully explained in Chapter 70 of my book: *How To Get Whatever You Want.*

But, beginning right now, start using the 3-G Method:

(1G) *Always express GRATITUDE*
(2G) *Always express GOODWILL*
(3G) *Always express GOOD WISHES*

This will make you popular, successful and happy. *It will do even more!*

It also will make you rich! Years ago, I personally lost several business opportunities which would have been worth a fortune—principally because I failed to express gratitude, goodwill and good wishes on *every* possible occasion, which would have included the *"right"* occasions . . . to the *"right"* people . . . at the *"right"* time.

I since have learned that this is no little thing —*but a great, big MUST!*

I earnestly recommend it to you.

But note that you must express gratitude, goodwill and good wishes to *every person* with whom you talk and to whom you write—*on every occasion.*

By doing this *constantly—without exception*— it will become a happy habit, a *constant personality plus* which will make you popular, successful and happy *throughout your entire life!*

Equally important (perhaps *more* important) is that by expressing gratitude, goodwill and good wishes to *every* person *without exception*—you will radiate happiness and goodwill to *all* others, without deliberately seeking any selfish gain from each, but just *the happiness it will give them.*

Yet, no matter how unselfishly you do it, you cannot plant seeds without reaping a harvest.

"As you sow, so shall you reap."

Chapter 44

Here's HELP! ...

It Is More Blessed To Give...
AND Receive

The Bible teaches, "It is more blessed to give *than to receive.*"

That, of course, is a profound truth which has come ringing down through the centuries. The world would be better, if more people heeded it.

The true art of giving is in not expecting— *and not wanting*—anything in return.

But there is an even greater art.

It is the art of giving—*and graciously accepting something in return.*

Do not receive that something, whatever it might be, for your *own* benefit—but to provide the person who received your gift, the satisfaction of giving you something (no matter how token) in return.

Do not give, *expecting* gratitude, but if gratitude or response is offered, accept it graciously.

This is not just an act of good manners, but an act of deep psychological importance.

Giving, even if entirely unselfish (and it too often is not)—is *patronage* and, as *patronage,* it can plant in the subconscious mind of the receiver a feeling of subservience which can grow into resentment.

Subconsciously, the recipient of the gift feels a sense of obligation, of silent "debt".

Unless the giver secretly provides the opportunity and enables the recipient to maintain pride by "canceling" the "debt" of patronage, the implied subservience and subconscious resentment may grow. And the intended good turns unintentionally bad.

By no means, need the expression of gratitude —tangible, spoken, or written—be remotely equal to the tangible value of the gift. But it should be graciously received as appropriately "equal".

The important—and often very impelling— psychological "need" of the recipient of a gift is that he or she received *AND gave in return.* And that the return gift was received graciously and appreciatively *as equal to or better than* the original gift.

Examples of "return gifts" of gratitude are countless, but we shall list a few:

The little child who appreciatively paints a tin can to make a flower vase as a "return gift" of gratitude.

The old lady who crochets a gift of appreciation and love.

The person who thanks you with such genuine appreciation that you feel repaid a hundred times.

The list of examples could go on and on. Because people of worth and character really *do* want to respond in their own appropriate way.

And you should let them.

Make sure they know that you feel "more than repaid" for your initial generosity. There is an art in receiving "return gifts" of gratitude.

In *giving AND receiving,* you replace patronage (and the possible resentment of unpaid obligation) with the self-esteem and pride of *mutual exchange* which provides fulfillment in subconscious "equality".

It is more blessed to give.

But it is blessed to receive, too, when you make the *receiving of gratitude* a gift, itself—a gift of self-esteem and pride.

For thus, you give *twice.*
And are twice blessed.

Chapter 45

Here's HELP! . . .

Be Like A Mighty River

A mighty river keeps moving forward to its known and charted destination. And it will get there.

It has dug its channel.

And so must you!

You must have a known and charted destination: *Your life-goal.* You must have a channel leading to your life-goal. And, like the mighty river, *keep moving forward in that channel.*

A mighty river may suffer the floods of adversity. *But always it returns to its channel.* And "keeps on rollin' along" to its destination.

And so must you!

You may, sometimes, suffer floods of adversity. But like the mighty river, *you must return to your channel* leading to success. And "keep on rollin' along" to your life-goal.

A mighty river has a current which varies.

Sometimes it moves forward faster than at other times. Sometimes with a great surge of power. Sometimes with calm serenity. But always the mighty river *moves forward* to its known and charted destination.

And so must you!

Like the mighty river, you will move forward slower at some times than at others. Do not let this disturb you any more than it disturbs the mighty river. The *speed* at which you move forward is not as important as the *constancy* of your moving forward to your life-goal.

The PROVEN SUCCESS METHOD of goal-achievement is *moving forward* in the *channel* you have charted to your goal.

So it will help you to think of your progress as a mighty river.

Get the "feel" of *constant forward movement.*

Get the "feel" of your life being *channeled* to your goal and the confidence that you will *stay in that charted channel.*

Get the "feel" of *a steady flow of mighty, unstoppable power*—as a natural consequence of channeled, forward movement to a definite objective.

It is important—psychologically—that you *do* have this *"mighty river feeling"*. Get the "feeling" that you *do* have a charted channel (*dug deep in your subconscious*) leading to your chosen life-goal.

Get the "feeling" of *a steady flow of constant, mighty, unstoppable movement forward* in that channel directly to your life-goal.

Continue re-reading this chapter until you get that *"feeling" and can arouse it intensely* whenever you want to. Which should be often!

Chapter 46

Here's HELP! . . .

You Cannot React Disagreeably If You Express Friendly, Good Humor

The title of this chapter is such a simple, obvious, indisputable fact that there would seem to be no reason to write more about it.

The reason for writing more about it is equally simple. It is this:

All people react disagreeably *part* of the time; *most* people react disagreeably *too much* of the time.

Why?

Again, the obvious, simple answer: People react disagreeably because they *disagree.*

And, *why* do they disagree?

Because other people (and the world is full of "other people") *are not exact duplicates of ourselves.* The old cliché that "no two people are alike" is true—fortunately or unfortunately, depending upon your point of view . . . *and your disposition.*

Not being exactly like you—and, perhaps, *being very different*—"other people" do not always think and act as *you* would and as you would like *them* to.

You can react in three ways:

(1) *You can react disagreeably.* You can quietly (and, of course, conspicuously) sulk. Or you can make a noisy and unpleasant major production out of your disagreement. Or settle for some form of expressing your disagreement in between those two extremes.

Since the "way to be agreeable is to agree", it follows that *"the way to be disagreeable is to disagree".*

The fastest, surest way to acquire the unpopular reputation of being a disagreeable person is to disagree with almost everybody about almost everything.

Yet many people make a career of doing just that! They even *volunteer* their vocal disagreement when their opinion is neither asked nor wanted. *There is no surer way to be unpopular!*

(2) The second way to react when other people do not think and act as you would like them to—*is to be tolerant. (Not condescending—tolerant!)*

"Get involved!" has almost become a national slogan. Too many people take this to mean: "Get involved *disagreeably.*" Hence the organized and disorganized dissidents who plague almost all causes with their noisy dissent ranging from demonstrations to riots.

Dissent and disagreement have become our national pastimes and are threatening to become our national —and world—preoccupations.

It is high time we stopped seeking things about which to disagree and argue and resent and become angry.

160

Instead, let us seek areas of agreement, then let us expand those areas of agreement in a spirit of tolerance and goodwill.

Which brings us to the third of the three ways in which you can react when other people do not think and act as you would like them to.

(3) *Maintain a relaxed attitude of friendly, good humor.*

Earlier in this book, we noted some of the many uses of the *Law of Consistency* as applied to PROVEN SUCCESS METHODS.

Here is another valuable use of the *Law of Consistency:*

It is *not consistent*—and therefore *not possible* —for you to maintain a relaxed attitude of friendly, good humor and *at the same time* react disagreeably.

Thus you instantly DOUBLE your *personality attractiveness:*

(1) By not reacting disagreeably—you obviously do not project a disagreeable personality.

(2) By maintaining a *relaxed attitude of friendly, good humor*—you project the personality characteristics proven to be most effective in *breaking the "stranger-barrier" and establishing yourself as a welcome companion!*

And *that* will be just the beginning!

Chapter 47

Here's HELP! . . .

As They Say On Ocean Voyages: "Let's Have A HAPPY SHIP!"

The ideal of every ocean voyage is to have what is known to all seafarers as a *"happy ship"*.

That means that *all* of the officers, crew, and especially the passengers, are satisfied, cooperative, congenial and happy.

Mrs. Kopmeyer and I have been on a number of ocean cruises. The degree to which each ship was a *"happy ship"* was an intangible *something* which one could sense the first day out, and which became more "real" with each passing day. All of our cruises were very enjoyable— that was their purpose—but, even then there was a "happy ship" difference.

There is something about *"everybody being in the same boat"* which especially requires the mutual satisfaction, cooperation, congeniality and pleasantness of *everybody aboard*.

But on the space-ship *"Earth"*, less than one-fourth of the passengers travel in what might reasonably be described as "First Class", while more than three-fourths of all the passengers on the space-ship *"Earth"* have to travel in the crowded poor accommodations of steerage.

So, on our one and only *"Earth Ship"* voyage, we do not have a *"happy ship"*.

We cannot change this by instantly moving the three-fourths of the passengers from "steerage" to "First Class".

Such vast resources and implementations simply are not available. Nor, are most of the "steerage" passengers sufficiently motivated to acquire the education, skilled job-training and adaptability to drastically changed living standards to accept mass opportunities for rapid advancement, even if such opportunities could be provided on such a massive scale.

I have been in foreign countries where underprivileged, under-educated, under-motivated parts of the population were offered low-cost or free modern apartments if they would move from their wood and mud huts. They adamantly would not. The modern, "renewal" apartments remained empty. The under-motivated people remained in their wood and mud huts.

The under-motivated people complain about their poor accommodations but *they will not accept greatly advanced change.*

We can and must make *gradual improvements at a rate acceptable to the slowly motivated.* And we must try to increase their motivation so that more rapid progress will be acceptable.

Especially, we must provide unlimited oppor-

tunities for *all* the motivated people who are eager for progress and willing to earn the improvements which we must make available.

Always, social movements must be upward. Never should they be lowered.

Nothing (but mass destruction!) would be accomplished on space-ship "Earth", by attempting to move the "First Class" passengers to "steerage" in the ideology of "mass equality".

Nor will *anyone* benefit if some radical steerage passengers blow up the section of the ship now designated "First Class". Because we "all are in the same boat", if one part is destroyed and sinks, the entire ship—and everybody—sinks with it.

Well? What to do?

First, *all* of the passengers have to *accept some basic facts:*

(1) We are—*all* of us—*"in the same boat".* Whether some of the passengers like it or not, we are—*all* of us—going to make our one and only *"Earth Ship"* voyage *together.*

It surely is time for *all* of us to *accept* the fact of being *together*—and stop *pretending* that we are *separate because we are different.* Certainly, *each* of us is *different.* And just as certainly, *all* of us are *together!*

(2) We will—*all* of us—have a more pleasant *one-and-only* trip, if we—*all* of us—*try much harder* to make our space-ship "Earth" a "happy ship".

Sometimes, it seems as if many of the passengers (and the officers and crew) are making frequent (or constant!) efforts to make space-ship "Earth" an unhappy ship!

Too many people work too hard at being divisive! Yet, we are *"all in the same boat"* on the same— and *only*—voyage. It seems incredible that *everyone* should not do *everything* possible to make our *only* ship— a *"happy ship"*—on our *only* voyage!

(3) We are going to have to greatly improve —immediately for the now-motivated and gradually for the slowly-motivated—the crowded, poor accommodations of the three-fourths of the passengers now in "steerage". *And we are not now making even a token effort to do this!* To the contrary, we are thinking in terms of 3-day work-weeks, production quotas, food-crop limitations, much earlier retirement—*and our schemes for doing less and less are the only things we are increasing!*

We should be *doubling* our efforts, working *twice* as hard, *twice* as long—and *ten times* more intelligently!

We should be thinking, not of *sparing* ourselves, but of *sharing* ourselves!

This is not an advocacy of socialism.

It is not an advocacy of *"free"* enterprise, either.

It is an advocacy of *full* enterprise, *full* production, *full* employment, *full* services, *full* opportunity— for *everybody* on our space-ship *"Earth"* on this, our *only* voyage!

Starting right NOW! With *everybody* thinking, working, cooperating to *make it happen!* To make *"Earth"* a *"happy ship"*!

It *can* happen, you know. It is just that we haven't *really tried!*

Chapter 48

Here's HELP! . . .

You May Be Sorry You Stirred It!

The waiter asked an unhappy looking customer what he found wrong with the soup.

The unhappy customer sadly replied, *"I'm sorry I stirred it!"*

There will be many situations in your life which *you will regret having stirred!*

So let us leave the unhappy customer with his unappetizing soup, which he made more unappetizing by his having *stirred* it—and let us consider more serious situations in life which you will regret having *stirred.*

Advice against stirring up trouble dates back more than 2,000 years. There was a Roman poet of those days who wrote more common sense than most philosophers of that vaunted age of wisdom. His name was Plautus. *He strongly advised against stirring up a hornets' nest*—2,000 years ago!

Yet 2,000 years later, people still seem impelled to stir up hornets' nests of trouble!

In my book, *Thoughts to Build On,* I wrote a chapter titled: "The Gentle Art Of Letting Alone". It is an art which everyone should learn and thus avoid much unnecessary trouble.

In these days of unrestrained activism, the slogan is: *"Get Involved!"* People, especially the young and inexperienced, rush, heedless of consequences, to *get involved* in every cause!

It matters not that the "cause" of the movement was professionally *stirred up* by those who make profitable careers of *stirring up "causes"* for others to get involved in—then leave those others *involved in the stirring.*

And if the "cause" turns out to be a hornets' nest, who gets "stung" while *stirring* it?

Eager-beaver YOU! That's who!

There are many worthy causes which urgently need your active involvement. *And this is not to urge non-involvement,* but to advise *selective* involvement and involvement which is *concentrated* in those worthy projects in which *you can render a tangible personal service of consequence.*

Too many people feel that they have made a significant contribution merely by being "among the demonstrators". There is more to service than providing a body to be counted in the statistics.

Consider these common sense rules:

(1) Select a worthy cause in which your involvement will be a *tangible, personal service of consequence.*

(2) Do not allow yourself to be "recruited" to stir a hornets' nest selected by a "career" trouble maker.

167

(3) Learn the "Gentle Art of Letting Alone". Remember, you may be sorry you *stirred* it!

Except for "career" trouble makers, most people do not *deliberately* stir up hornets' nests of trouble.

Yet, psychologists have discovered that most of people's personal troubles can be traced back to something the people, themselves, *did, said* or *wrote* sometime in the past.

In almost every case, the unpleasantness, controversy, or trouble would not have developed if the person had not, himself, *initiated* it—or *escalated* it.

The daily opportunities for such trouble-involvement *are concealed in "harmless" trivialities*—and here are a few:

Of course, you did not *intend* to cause the hurt feelings . . . which became resentment . . . then anger . . . then retaliation.

You merely expressed *"your adverse opinion"*.

Or, you volunteered *"constructive criticism"*.

Or, you forthrightly *"took sides"*.

Or, you merely said a *"witty thing at a tempting moment"*.

Or, you escalated a *"trivial disagreement"*.

Yes, *little* things; harmless trivialities.

BUT . . . even a *little* stick can stir up a hornets' nest.

And you may be sorry you stirred it!

Chapter 49

Here's HELP! . . .

Have You Thought About QUASARS Lately?

Do you think the job of succeeding is *too big?*

When the going gets rough, you can't stand the *heat?*

Does your life-goal seem *too far away?*

The QUASARS will make such *little* problems seem *so small* you will take them on with the confidence and assurance of a person who can put *little problems in proper perspective*—and thus handle them with ease.

Just *thinking* about QUASARS will make *all* of your problems *insignificant!*

So . . . think about QUASARS:

QUASARS are the most distant objects yet discovered in the Universe. These super space-objects were discovered by astronomers in 1963 and by now more than 200 QUASARS have been exactly located.

If you think your *life-goal* is too far away—compare its distance with QUASARS.

QUASARS are 54,000,000,000,000,000,000,000 miles away!

In a Universe so vast, the distance to your *life-goal* is infinitesimal! If your fellow humans can *see* QUASARS and *exactly locate them* at such great distances —surely you can see, exactly locate and, in a *comparatively* short time, reach your life-goal!

And if the going gets rough on the way to your life-goal, and you feel you *"can't stand the heat"* (as President Truman phrased it), compare that *"heat"* with QUASARS.

A QUASAR radiates *heat* 10,000,000,000,000 *times that of our sun!* And that is *really* hot!

So when your own going gets so rough that you think you *"can't stand the heat"*—compare that *"heat"* with QUASARS!

Then, realize that QUASARS which *man can see* 54,000,000,000,000,000,000,000 *miles away,* and which radiate *heat which is* 10,000,000,000,000 *times as hot as our sun*—are *only a tiny part of Infinity* which is *unlimited* space, *unlimited* time, *unlimited* power, *unlimited* knowledge, *unlimited everything!*

Like QUASARS—*you are a part of that Infinity!*

Your own subconscious mind is a part of the Infinite Mind and can channel into your life *whatever* you need to achieve your life-goal. (Now is an ideal time to re-read the first part of this book which teaches you HOW you can channel *Infinite Power* into *your* life.)

Infinite Power which furnishes radiant power equal to 10,000 *billion* of our suns to just *one* QUASAR—*obviously can furnish all of the means and power YOU need to achieve your life-goal and get whatever you want in life!*

If you do not yet realize and understand HOW *you* can channel *Infinite Power* into *your* life, then you have missed or not thoroughly understood the *first lessons of this book.*

Even if it is necessary for you to *read and re-read* the first series of chapter-lessons of this book *many times*—your learning HOW to channel *Infinite Power* into *your life* will be worth *any* amount of time and effort required.

Nothing is more important than your doing THAT!

Chapter 50

Here's HELP! . . .

The Past Is GONE!

You only can *live* in the *present;* the past is GONE!

If you will remember and constantly repeat this statement, it will make a profound change in your life.

You only can live in the present.

The past is GONE!

You cannot *live* in the past. You can cherish past joys. You may not entirely forget past sorrows. But you must think of *past* joys and *past* sorrows as *past events* —as *memories, not present emotions.*

This is one of the important lessons of successful, happy, sensible living: *Past* joys and *past* sorrows are PAST. And the *past* is GONE! Close the door.

Past joys and *past* sorrows are MEMORIES. *Do not reincarnate them as PRESENT EMOTIONS!*

You must totally accept the fact that the PAST IS GONE! *The past is memory! Only the present exists NOW!*

You may *remember* the past—*as past*. But *you cannot re-live* the past. You *cannot change* the past. You only can *live* in the present.

Your past mistakes are GONE with the past. Some of the *consequences* of past mistakes may carry over into the present—to be dealt with in the present. But your past mistakes are GONE with the past. You cannot *re-live* the event with a *second chance* to do better.

You can *learn* from your past mistakes as you would learn from any historical events. But such learning should be *intellectual*—*not emotional*. Just as you would study *any history*.

People who *emotionalize memories* of past grief, mistakes and resentment—add to their difficulties with the present. Inevitably, it is those who *emotionalize memories* of past unhappiness who have the most unhappiness in the present. Of course they do! *Emotionalizing an unhappy past assures an unhappy present.*

The past is GONE!

Close the door!

And open the door on a *present filled with opportunities you can do something about*—because *present* opportunities are "NOW"!

And "NOW" is all there *really* is!

Chapter 51

Here's HELP! . . .

So You Have Made Mistakes?
That's GOOD! Keep It Up!

The world belongs to those who *find out* what
will not work and, therefore, by elimination, discover what
will work.

If you make a career of doing those two things
—*both* of them—your success is assured.

*You can write any amount you want on your
pay checks!*

You see, that is what success is all about: (1)
finding out what *will not* work, and (2) by elimination, dis-
covering what *will* work.

Often, you can learn both: (1) what *will not*
work, and (2) what *will* work—*from those who already
know.* That is the best, fastest, least expensive way.

But there are times when such information is
not available to you (for many reasons), so you have to
blaze new trails.

You have to learn from your own experience—
including your own failures.

Charles Kettering, the great inventive genius
of automotive engineering, said that an inventor (and he
could have added "any progressive person who tries to
find out") *is almost always failing.*

Specifically, Charles Kettering said, "An inventor is *almost always failing*—he tries and *fails* maybe a
thousand times. *Our biggest job is to teach how to fail intelligently—to keep on trying and failing, and failing and
trying.*"

Then Charles Kettering, who probably more
than anyone else is responsible for the multi-billion dollar
General Motors corporate empire, explained *how to fail
intelligently:*

(1) Keep on trying and failing, and failing
and trying.

(2) No matter how often you fail—*do not
suffer any ego damage because of frequent failures.*

The *"instant failures"* become *"permanent failures"* because their first few failures *hurt their tender egos!*

The *"instant failures"* fail a few times and suffer *ego damage,* so they get discouraged and quit. Thus
they become *permanent failures.*

The *"quick quitters"* mentally panic as soon as
they fail a *few* times. They withdraw into their cozy cocoon
of nothingness because, having failed a *few* times, their
tender egos are hurt and they *fear that they can never
succeed* (in the kind of system in which *millions of people
are succeeding every day!*)

Those of us who actually have failed *thousands*

of times in the necessary process of *finding out what would not work* in order to learn *what would work*—wish we could explain the *necessity of failing hundreds or even thousands of times* to the "instant failures" who whine and panic if they fail a *few* times.

Failure is one of the most effective methods you can use to succeed!

Failure should not be feared and avoided; failure should be accepted and used!

In one of my books, *How To Get Whatever You Want* is an entire chapter devoted to "How To Fail Your Way To Success!" That one chapter may change your entire life! Certainly, it contains one of the important lessons of how to get whatever you want, because learning to *"fail intelligently"*, as Charles Kettering said, is one of the keys to success.

While you must not let failing hurt your ego, *neither must you let mistakes constantly nag you with a sense of guilt.*

This is not to condone *"deliberate mistakes"*, which are not "mistakes" at all but *deliberate wrongdoing.*

It is not intelligent, it is not commendable, it is not moral—*to do what you know or even believe to be wrong.*

Deliberate wrongdoing deserves the *inevitable sense of guilt* which is its certain consequence.

As any psychiatrist will assure you, the *sense of guilt* which inevitably results from *deliberate wrongdoing* is far greater than any possible self-gratification or "benefit". And do not try to rationalize that this is not or will not be so!

However, this does not apply to the countless mistakes in all lives which are *not deliberate wrongdoings,* but which are the natural consequence of not being perfect —and, of course, no human is.

No one should suffer ego damage or a sense of guilt because of *"honest mistakes"* which are the result of the valuable learning process of "testing" to find out what will not work so that, by elimination, one finally discovers what will work.

Such "testing" failures are statistical—not deliberately immoral. No sense of guilt is involved, but instead a sense of accomplishment because you will be *one step closer* to finding out what *will* work—*and success!*

Thomas Edison devoted *ten years of continuing "mistakes"* before he found the *right* way to make the nickel-iron-alkaline storage battery.

Edison and his staff tested and classified *17,000 varieties of plants* before they succeeded in extracting latex in substantial quantities from just *one* of them! When *you* are willing to make *17,000 "mistakes" or failures* in order to *succeed once*—you will have learned the necessity for and the value of "mistakes" and failures!

Edison *failed* more than anyone else. As a result, he knew more things that *wouldn't work* than anyone else. So with that kind of information, he *succeeded* more than anyone else! He patented 1,093 inventions worth millions!

Is *your* fear of making mistakes keeping YOU from being a *big success?*

Chapter 52

Here's HELP! . . .

Do Not Use "Baby Methods"
On Adult Problems

When a baby wants something: food, comfort, attention—the baby *cries*.

If crying does not produce instant, free assistance from "someone", the baby *yells* at the top of its voice.

This usually brings the "someone" to give the desired free assistance. *And the baby subconsciously remembers.*

Thus, this natural and often necessary infant instinct continues into childhood. The young child, not yet having learned logical persuasion, continues to use *crying* as a means of "calling attention" to wants—and *yelling* as a means of "demanding".

Parents, by compliantly responding to the child's *crying* and *yelling*, reinforce the subconscious memory of these *"baby methods"* as the effective means of getting wants freely fulfilled by "somebody".

As such indulged children grow into adolescence, their egos will not permit "baby crying", so they substitute complaining and defiance. Their yelling usually is confined to group shouting—increasingly of "demands".

Or they demonstrate their "suffering from denial" by withdrawal or anti-social acts.

And they grow into adults whose training from infancy has been a long sequence of first expected, then tolerated—infantile, childish, adolescent means of *"calling attention"* to and ultimately *"demanding"* instant, free assistance from "somebody".

This is not a condemnation solely of our present generation—although our present generation has produced some notable examples of this form of childish behavior in adults.

By the very nature of its instinctive beginning —the quite proper attending the needs of a crying baby— every generation since the beginning of civilization has had its proportion of adolescents and adults who sought to alleviate their "grievances" and have their wants satisfied by their using childish behavior.

What is the result?

As individuals, they become the *problem-people* of each generation. They *react inadequately* to even normal situations or they *over-react in many disagreeable ways* to every imagined threat to their tender egos which their parents, then their associates and always they, themselves, have pampered and over-protected throughout the sequent stages of their lives.

In groups, they become *people-problems:* as aggressive demonstrators, militant protestors, picketing boycotters and destructive disrupters.

These are adolescent and adult exhibitions of

179

of childish behavior. When these problem-people were babies, they cried as their means of "calling attention"—*and "someone" responded.*

When these problem-people were young children, they yelled as their means of "demanding"—*and "somone" responded.*

Childish behavior became established in their subconscious as their effective means of getting "someone" to provide attention and free assistance. And so they continued it through adolescence and into adult life.

Babies, children, adolescents and adults will continue to use childish behavior as long as it is effective in getting "someone" to provide attention and free assistance.

Sometime, in the various stages of growing up, every person needs to be taught that *the methods of childish behavior are no longer effective* in achieving goals.

Then, people will stop using *"baby methods"* on adult problems.

The Bible tells that *when Jesus became a man, He "put away all childish things".*

It was *when* He put away all childish things, that *"Jesus increased in wisdom and stature and in favor with God and man."*

So it must be with each of us. We must put away all childish things—*especially childish behavior*—before we can become mature, effective goal-achieving adults.

Chapter 53

Here's HELP! ...

Families Who Laugh And Play Together—STAY Together

Theologians long have preached: "Families who *pray* together—*stay* together."

That is a proven fact. It need not be expanded here.

This chapter will provide two other ways to hold families together.

At a time in history when the family, the cornerstone of social stability, is disintegrating, *we need every means available to preserve family unity*—or, more informally, family togetherness.

It is not our purpose here to analyse the sociological breakdown of the family as a durable, secure social unit.

Especially, we shall not blame it all on the over-emphasized "generation-gap," because the breech is equally wide within the *same* generation. For example, husband and wife, where statistics show increasing incompatibility leading to "escape" through divorce. This is not due to a *"generation gap"* but to an *"understanding gap."*

In so serious a matter, one should not propose frivolous solutions, yet I wish to recommend two—which are not as frivolous as they may, at first, seem. See for yourself:

(1) Families who *laugh together—STAY together.*

Good humor—*affectionate and imperturbable good humor*—removes the friction which wears apart the bonds of family unity.

So, we rely again on the *Law of Consistency.* It is *impossible* to be angry, resentful, intolerant or to maintain any of the disagreeable attitudes which are so destructive of family harmony—*in the presence of affectionate good humor.* It would be *inconsistent* and, therefore, is *impossible.*

Maintaining good humor as a constant personality trait and often joyously expressing it with *laughter* will make a happy family—especially if the personality traits of good humor and laughter are instilled and encouraged in *every* member of the family. It is a help that good humor and laughter are contagious.

Obviously, criticism and nagging are not conducive to happy family life. Neither are ill-tempered arguments. Yet, it is within the family that these most often take place.

How much better it would be if family life were filled with affectionate good humor and homes were joyous with laughter!

Families who *laugh together—STAY together.*

And, as a sequence, the second happy solution:

(2) Families who *play together—STAY together!*

Certainly, the members of the family should *love* each other. And *show* it!

But, it is almost as important that the members should *like* each other, *like* being *with* each other . . . and *like* being *together!*

Each member of the family should try at least as hard to be *popular* with all of the other members of the family as with outside groups. Yet, this seldom is so. The family is too often taken for granted while outside groups are cultivated with personality plus!

If Dad would be as cordial and genial at home as at the Rotary Club!

If Mom would be as entertaining at home as she is at the Woman's Club!

If daughter would try as hard to be Miss Personality at home as at the school pageant!

If Junior would be a cheer leader at home, too!

Well . . . that might be a little *much!* Or, *would* it?

Anyway, home should not just be where you let your hair down; home should be where you let your *care* down, too! *And have fun!*

Families should have *fun* . . . *together!* Home should be a *fun place!*

You fill in the details. But it is so necessary, yet so neglected, I want to say it again:

Families who *play together—STAY together!*

Chapter 54

Here's HELP! . . .

Always Make Everyone Feel Better Because Of YOU!

This chapter may provide the key to your greatest satisfaction in life!

Especially if you really try to do this with *everyone* at *every* opportunity:

ALWAYS MAKE EVERYONE FEEL BETTER . . . BECAUSE OF YOU!

Whenever you *talk* with anyone, *say* something which will make that person *feel better!* A sincere compliment . . . inspiring encouragement . . . repeating a favorable comment made by another . . . your expression of gratitude, goodwill, good wishes! There are *dozens* of different things to *say* to make others *feel better!*

Make a list of all of the different kinds of things you can *say* to another to make that person *feel better*. Review your list often so that you will do this automatically *every time* you *talk* to *anyone*.

This applies to talking in person or by telephone. Whenever and however you *talk* to another—*always* make that person *feel better* because of YOU!

This also applies to speaking to groups in small, informal talks, or in major public speeches in person or over radio or television. What you say to make your listeners *feel better* may be the most audience-satisfying part of your speech! The speakers who *always* make their listeners *feel better* are in great demand.

Yes, this applies to school classroom lectures, too! The teacher who can make every student *feel better* for having attended that class provides more than an academic lesson; that teacher provides mental-emotional therapy! The lesson may increase knowledge, but the mental-emotional therapy of *feeling better* improves *personalities and attitudes!*

Improved *attitudes* may be most important of all because, as Dr. Walter Scott, President of Northwestern University, said, "Success or failure is caused more by *mental attitudes* than by mental capacities."

In your personal and business correspondence, *write* something which will make the recipient *feel better*.

The *entire* content—for many reasons—may not be good news, but you should, at least, conclude your letter with a compliment . . . encouragement . . . a sincere expression of gratitude, goodwill, good wishes.

It may require a little additional thought and time for you *always* to make *everyone feel better because of YOU*—but I assure you it is *many times worth it!*

Not only will you make *everyone feel better* because of YOU . . . *but you will feel many times better, yourself!*

Chapter 55

Here's HELP! . . .

Maybe Life Is PINCHING Them!

That great, old Roman biographer, Plutarch, wrote about a man who had suddenly become irritable and short-tempered.

When his associates criticized his disagreeable conduct, the man showed them a fine, new shoe.

Holding the shoe for his critics to examine closely, the man asked his critics, "Is this shoe not well made and of fine quality?"

His critics agreed that the shoe was, indeed, well made and of fine quality and appearance.

Then the man observed, "But by *only looking at* this shoe, you cannot know that it PINCHES my foot and thus makes me uncomfortable and irritable."

Life is like that shoe, sometimes.

Because the lives of others may appear *on the surface* to be fine and attractive, we do not realize that, somewhere, life may be PINCHING them.

We cannot know from the outside—that others may be *hurting* inside.

So before you judge others too quickly and too critically for their being irritable or rude—remember that life may be PINCHING them somewhere.

It does not help their hurt for you to be critical or resentful. Certainly, it does not help *you!*

So *always assume* that if another is irritable or disagreeable, life is PINCHING them somewhere. Then *treat* them as someone who has been or is being *hurt*. Treat them with kindness and understanding, with tolerance and sympathy.

You both will be better for it!

Chapter 56

Here's HELP! . . .

Are You A Thermometer . . .
Or A Thermostat?

Many people are like a thermometer.

A thermometer does not *change* anything. It does not *control* anything. A thermometer is simply a convenience to people who may happen to want the limited information (service) which it can provide.

Many people are like a thermometer. They do not *change* anything. They do not *control* anything. They merely exist to provide a limited service as a convenience to others.

Like a thermometer, these people *are affected by what happens*. Like a thermometer, what *happens*, within the range of their comprehension, shows on their faces. But like a thermometer, *these people do not do anything about what happens*.

Other people are like a thermostat.

A thermostat is constantly alert to what happens and it *does whatever is required to adjust conditions according to a pre-determined plan.*

A thermostat *manages its environment* to meet changed conditions. A thermostat is in *control.* It does not accept conditions which are contrary to its objective; *it acts instantly to change them* to comply with a predetermined plan.

A thermometer *exists.*

A thermostat *controls.*

You can be like a thermometer . . . merely exist . . . change nothing . . . control nothing . . . just serve, within limited capabilities, as a convenience to people if they happen to be interested.

Or you can be like a thermostat . . . constantly alert to what happens . . . acting instantly to maintain control . . . changing any condition which is not in accordance with a predetermined plan.

The kind of person you will become need not be determined by your present situation. *Unless you let it!*

Your life need not be dominated or controlled by others. *Unless you permit them!*

You cannot be denied the abundance of whatever you want. *Unless you refuse to use proven success methods!*

The choice is yours—and yours alone!
You can be whatever you want to be!
You can have whatever you want to have!
You can do whatever you want to do!
The choice is yours—and *yours alone!*
You can be like a *thermometer!*
Or, you can be like a *thermostat!*

Chapter 57

Here's HELP! . . .

"If You Can't Stand The Heat..."

No, this isn't going to be about former President Harry Truman's much-quoted remark: "If you can't stand the heat—get out of the kitchen."

Anyway, I think he got the idea from my boxing coach: "If you're afraid of getting hit—stay out of the ring."

But the purpose of this chapter *is to discuss halos*. Especially the inferior stuff out of which many people are making their own personal imaginary halos, these days.

People in all walks of life—from the near-great to the not-so-great—have gone into the personal halo-making business. These self-made halos are worn in the wearers' own imagination as self-righteous symbols of their own goodness and their self-publicized good deeds, whether in the family group, or social service organizations, or in churches, clubs or wherever their halos provide self-gratification.

There seems to be an ever-increasing number of people who put on their self-made halos and go forth to champion good causes. Good causes need all the leaders—*and workers*—they can get, but I am in favor of leaders who give the credit—and the publicity—*to the workers*. I have no admiration for those who speak for the poor and underprivileged by using the backs of the poor and underprivileged as a podium for personal image-building.

There are those who "prove" their leadership by conspicuously marching in front—especially for television. In fact, next to inflammatory statements, television is the great leadership image builder. And, television has made it so by its own choice of subjects.

Television—and radio and the press—would do a greater public service to devote less time and space to pompous (or inflammatory) statements of television-built leaders, and *devote more time and space to the statements, opinions and situations of those whose problems need to be solved* and to those who are working at the *grass roots* to solve them.

This would create an informed and activated public. It also would relieve the monotony of the leadership image building with which television and other media seem to be obsessed.

Until that enlightened and interesting change of focus, we have one consolation: *As the public spotlight gets brighter and hotter—the self-made, ersatz halos of some publicity-built leaders begin to wilt.*

And nothing looks sillier than a would-be leader with a self-made halo which wilted when the going got hot!

Chapter 58

Here's HELP! ...

"Take" It ... Or Leave It!

In the preceding chapter, I mentioned former President Harry Truman's much-quoted advice: "If you can't stand the heat—*get out of the kitchen.*"

It is good advice. It might be re-phrased more literally: "If you can't 'take' it—*leave it.*"

And, I would like to suggest that if you get involved in an *intolerable* situation which you *can't "take"*— *then leave it!*

That doesn't sound very heroic, does it? Well, continuing to butt your head against a stone wall may show perserverance, it may show your capacity to endure pain, but it is not heroic either—merely stupid.

However, being ready, willing and able to "take" the *bearable* blows which life will inevitably pound upon you is necessary if you are to maintain a stable personality in a world in which each of us is allotted a share of troubles, disappointments and heartaches. So you must be able to "take" it. When *unavoidable* trouble besets you, you must calmly "take" it in stride by doing four things— the 4 A'S:

(1) ADMIT that the trouble does exist. Don't try to pretend it isn't so, *if it is.*

(2) ACCEPT it—*if it is inevitable*—as one of the vicissitudes of life.

(3) ADJUST to it. The ability to *adjust to change,* especially unpleasant change, is one of the most important characteristics of a successful personality.

(4) ACT to improve the situation. *There is something you can do to improve on almost every situation.* Find out what it is and do it at once. Continuous, intelligent action will allieviate depression—and create solutions.

Those four actions—taken in that order—will enable you to handle, in the best possible way, almost any *unavoidable* trouble that comes along. You'll be able to "take" it.

Developing determination backed by mental and physical toughness and a sure spiritual faith will reinforce your capacity to "take" it when trouble is *inevitable.*

But most trouble is not inevitable! You can decide whether it is in your own best interest to "take" it— *or leave it!*

There is strong character-building in meeting trouble head on. It is beneficial exercise in building mental and physical toughness. It offers an opportunity to develop spiritual faith.

As long as "taking" trouble is a method of mastering and eliminating it, and an exercise in problem-solving and character-building—by all means, "take" it. As long as there is a feeling of exhilaration in meeting challenges and overcoming difficulties—welcome them. That's part of the fun of living!

However, when you use trouble to make you feel that you are being a martyr or to impress others with your martyrdom in order to invoke their sympathy and perhaps obtain their favors, you are, to that extent, psychotic and need help by those qualified to treat your psychosis.

In the beginning of this chapter we said, "Take it—*or leave it*." We have discussed "taking" trouble. Now, when should you leave it? Of course, there is no set rule. Each personal situation is different.

But you don't have to butt your head against a stone wall to show your perseverance or your capacity to endure pain or to establish a martyr image. *If you are, in fact, up against a stone wall, don't butt it—leave it!* There are a number of "stone walls" in every life and there may be one in yours which can break you if you persist in continuously butting it. *Just leave it!*

What are these "stone walls" which one should leave rather than butt. Here are a few examples:

Somewhere, along the maze of life's highways, perhaps recently, perhaps long ago, you took the wrong road. It seemed to be the road to take at the time, but now blocking your path to happiness and success—is a stone wall. *Leave* that *wrong* road; seek the *right* road.

You may be involved, intolerably, in the wrong career. *Leave it!* You may be working, with insufficient reward or opportunity, in the wrong business. *Leave it!* The stone wall in many couples' lives is an incompatible marriage. *Leave it!* You may be associating with a group which offers you neither stimulating conversation, nor enjoyable experiences, nor worthwhile companionship. *Leave it!*

Just remember, when trouble comes your way, *you have a choice*—you can "take" it or leave it. Whichever you do will depend on the circumstances and your own thoughtful judgment.

Don't think, for one minute, that choosing to leave an intolerable situation will brand you a coward. It is often more courageous, and usually more intelligent, to "leave it," to go on to more rewarding experiences, than it is to wreck yourself against one of your "stone walls" because you are afraid of what someone may think if you don't choose to stupidly "take" it.

Don't be afraid to "leave" it!

Don't "stay in the kitchen" if "taking the heat" *isn't worth it!*

Chapter 59

Here's HELP! . . .

Being Successful Is So EASY That ANYBODY Can Do It!

Psychologist, Dr. Emile Coué, gave all of his patients the following mental prescription: "Always *think* of what you have to do as EASY and it will *become* so."

That mental prescription of Dr. Coué applies especially to *being successful*.

Always think of *being successful* as EASY.

Because it is!

Being successful is EASY—provided that you understand "EASY" to mean: *"so simple that anybody can obtain, understand, learn and use PROVEN SUCCESS METHODS which assure success."*

Being successful is EASY—provided that you understand "EASY" to mean that PROVEN SUCCESS METHODS are *not difficult* to obtain, understand, learn or use.

In fact, I cannot think of *even one* PROVEN

SUCCESS METHOD which is *too difficult* for *any* person to obtain *easily* . . . to understand *easily* . . . to learn *easily* . . . to use *easily* . . . with the *certain result* that the person doing so will *succeed easily.*

To be entirely factual, I must add that there are a *few* persons who are so tragically retarded—mentally or emotionally—that success, in their cases, is a matter of degree. Those *few* exceptions are clinical cases and are not the object of this chapter.

But, with those *few* tragic exceptions, *every* person—including *all* of the other *hundreds of millions* of Americans—*can succeed EASILY!*

This includes the *millions* of *presently* under-motivated, under-privileged, under-educated men, women and teen-agers—*any or all of whom can succeed EASILY!*

Success does not depend upon *where you are NOW*—success depends upon *where you are going!*

Success does not depend upon *what you are NOW*—success depends upon *what you are becoming!*

Anybody can have a *successful life-goal!* And, achieve it EASILY!

Remember that "EASILY," as used here, does *not* mean "lazily," or "indifferently," or "without intense thought and effort."

You cannot be successful—*"lazily,"* or *"indifferently,"* or *"without intense thought and effort."*

You *can* be successful EASILY—because there are *hundreds* of PROVEN SUCCESS METHODS, and *every proven success method* is EASY for *every person* to *obtain* . . . to *understand* . . . to *learn* . . . and to *use* . . . with the *certain* result of *succeeding EASILY!*

Millions of people have somehow been led (or misled) to *believe* that success is *too difficult for them.* They *believe* that they are too poor, too under-privileged, too under-educated, too handicapped by all sorts of limitations to succeed *at all*—certainly not to succeed EASILY!

Millions of people have somehow been led (or misled) to *believe* that their *present* condition condemns them to lives of poverty or mediocrity!

Nonsense! That just is not so!

Millions of Americans live in poverty or near-poverty for the simple reason that neither they nor the people who are paid to "help" them—*use* PROVEN SUCCESS METHODS!

Yet, the PROVEN SUCCESS METHODS which the poor *can* and *should* USE to lift themselves out of poverty—are so EASY to understand . . . so EASY to learn . . . so EASY to use . . . *that anybody can use them!* So *anybody* can succeed EASILY!

And that *"anybody"* includes not only the millions of poor, themselves, but also the thousands of welfare helpers *who do not know and, therefore, do not teach* PROVEN SUCCESS METHODS to the *presently* under-motivated, under-privileged, under-educated poor.

The poor deserve better success training than being taught to chant in unison: "I am POOR, but I am somebody." That makes them "somebody who is POOR".

The poor deserve the kind of success training which *replaces* the *negative goal-command* "I am POOR" with the *positive goal-command* "I will SUCCEED!"

That *positive goal-command* "I will SUCCEED!" repeated *thousands* of times, must be *materialized* by their being *taught* and *motivated to use* PROVEN SUC-CESS METHODS which result in increasing and certain success! EASY success!

The PROVEN SUCCESS METHODS which will change poverty (or mediocrity) into success are so EASY that *anybody*—including the millions of *presently* under-motivated, under-educated, under-privileged men, women and teen-agers—can EASILY *obtain* . . . EASILY *understand* . . . EASILY *learn* . . . and EASILY *use* the PROVEN SUCCESS METHODS which make personal success EASY . . . *and certain!*

Success is not getting more welfare aid; success is using PROVEN SUCCESS METHODS which make welfare aid unnecessary—and unwanted.

Being successful is so EASY that *anybody* can do it!

Being successful is so EASY that *everybody* should!

Chapter 60

Here's HELP! . . .

How To Succeed Just By Dropping Paper Clips Into A Cup!

Did you know that you can greatly increase your work-efficiency and your rate of success—*just by dropping paper clips into a cup?*

I use this *proven success method* every day and I can guarantee that it works!

Here's how I do it:

(1) I keep a cup of paper clips on my desk.

(2) Every morning, I scatter a handful of paper clips on my desk—just beyond the work-space, but in clear, *challenging* view!

(3) Then I put my day's work in front of me— arranged in the order in which I want to do it.

(4) I think intensely: "I shall take up *one* problem or task *at a time*" (then I pick up *one* paper clip, symbolic of the *one* problem or task).

(5) Then I think intensely: "I shall *dispose* of that problem or task *at once* (*then I drop the paper clip*

into the cup, symbolic of the disposal of the problem or task).

(6) Having thus "set the mental stage" for my *Paper Clip Concentration Game,* I take up the first problem or task of the day . . . *complete* it . . . *dispose* of it (and I remove *one* of the paper clips which I previously had scattered on my desk, and *drop it back into the cup—* symbolic of the disposal of *that* problem or task).

(7) Then I repeat the procedure with each problem or task . . . *in the proper order* . . . *one at a time* . . . (emphasizing its *disposal* by removing *one more paper clip* from my desk and dropping it emphatically back into the cup).

My simple *Paper Clip Concentration Game* is psychologically effective because:

(a) It focuses concentration on *disposing* of *one* problem or task *at a time.*

(b) The ever-visible *remaining* paper clips are a *challenging reminder* of more problems or tasks still remaining to be *disposed* of.

(c) The dropping of each paper clip into the cup emphasizes the *finality* of the *completion* of each job— for as the great psychologist, William James, taught: "When once a decision is reached and execution is the order of the day, dismiss absolutely all responsibility and care (anxiety) about the outcome."

When you drop each paper clip into the cup it signifies that the problem or task is *disposed* of with *finality.* It is *completed! Done! Finished!*

And . . . *on to the next job!*

That is HOW to get things *done!*

Chapter 61

Here's HELP! . . .

Do You Want To ATTRACT MONEY?

It is the title and the purpose of this book to provide HELP in the form of *proven success methods*.

Having devoted forty years of my life to researching, testing and compiling PROVEN SUCCESS METHODS, I retired to contribute my remaining years to publishing and distributing this vast treasure of PROVEN SUCCESS METHODS through my books, magazine articles and nationally syndicated newspaper articles which reach millions of readers.

Many of these readers have been so kind as to write me, and while "success" means many things to many people, I have found that most people include "money" as one of the elements of "success".

This is natural and proper since money provides the *means* and the *capability* to do many necessary and worthwhile deeds and services *which would be impossible without money*.

Most of the readers who write me about PROVEN SUCCESS METHODS for making a lot of money do not want more money just to hoard in an *inactive* bank account. *They want money as a means of accomplishing something worthwhile.*

So, as America's Success Counselor to millions, I shall continue to include in my PROVEN SUCCESS METHODS many, many ways to attract and acquire *money*—and when I use the word *"money"*, I mean a *lot of money!*

You will find that many of the chapter-lessons in this book and in my other books can be applied directly or indirectly to attracting and acquiring *money*—even though the chapter-lesson, itself, may not *specifically concentrate on money.*

However, in this chapter, *we shall specifically concentrate on MONEY.*

In fact, we shall use MONEY, itself, as a *psychological concentration object.* This is a PROVEN SUCCESS METHOD because in order to attract and acquire large sums of money, you must be *"money conscious".*

Financial advisors, economists, psychologists, success counselors—experts who know about attracting and acquiring large sums of money—all agree that being *"money conscious"* is a major essential.

Throughout this book, you will find many psychological methods of attracting and getting WHATEVER you want—*including MONEY.* You will find that one of the principal methods taught is for you to maintain a constant awareness—a *psychological consciousness* (through *mental pictures,* for example)—of WHATEVER you want . . . *and that applies to MONEY.*

You can use *mental pictures:* THINK RICH!

You can use a *goal command:* "MAKE A MIL-LION!"

You can use *concentration objects.* Some are listed in this book and a complete section of my book *How To Get Whatever You Want* is devoted to the most effective *concentration objects* for WHATEVER you want.

In this chapter, you will learn about the most effective *concentration object* for MONEY.

It is MONEY, itself!

It is a DOLLAR BILL BOOK MARK.

You now have in your hands, a book which will teach you many *proven success methods* for attracting and acquiring MONEY.

Now . . . DO THIS:

(1) Take a *dollar bill* (a new crisp dollar bill is best) and place it in this book so that approximately *two inches of the dollar bill will show at all times above the top of the book* as you read.

(2) Then, when you must stop reading, *use the dollar bill as a book mark* to mark the place where you want to begin reading at your next opportunity.

(3) You will be amazed at the "attention power" of your *dollar bill book mark!* At first, your *dollar bill book mark* will be a *conscious* "concentration object" and will command your *conscious* attention.

(4) Then, it will begin to make its "money conscious" impression on your *subconscious mind* and, gradually, your *subconscious mind* will take over the "concentration" so that your *always exposed* dollar bill book mark will not distract your conscious attention from your

reading—but it will be making intense, continuous impressions in your *goal-achieving subconscious!*

Using a DOLLAR BILL BOOK MARK as you read the PROVEN SUCCESS METHODS in this and my other books will give the methods greatly increased acceleration—*especially in attracting MONEY!*

You also can use the *coins* in your pocket or purse—as concentration objects—to ATTRACT MONEY!

Here's how to do it:

(1) Your objective is to become intensely *"money-conscious"* . . . to THINK RICH!

(2) By being *"money-conscious"* and THINKING RICH, you direct (or "computerize") your all-powerful subconscious to *direct you to* or *attract to you* the opportunities, personal contacts and means of acquiring great wealth.

(3) This use of your subconscious to get *whatever you want* is described in detail in various chapters and sections of this book, so we shall not repeat all of the methods here—but shall simply explain how to use coins to impress a powerful GOAL COMMAND into your subconscious.

(4) As our example, we shall use the goal command for WEALTH . . . *"Make a million!"*

(5) The method is to repeat your goal command for WEALTH . . . *"Make a million!"* over and over again (aloud if you are alone; silently to yourself if others are present).

(6) By repeating your goal command over and over, hundreds of times every day, you will intensely impress into your subconscious . . . *"Make a million! . . .*

Make a million! . . . Make a million! . . . Make a million!"

(7) By doing that over a period of weeks and months—you will become *"money-conscious"*. You will THINK RICH! And that's how you *attract money!*

(8) When you *handle money* at the same time you are repeating your goal command: *"Make a million!"* —you more intensely impress your goal command into your subconscious.

(9) So, hold from three to six coins in one hand. Then put one coin into your other hand and *forcefully* repeat your goal command *four times: "Make a million! . . . Make a million! . . . Make a million! . . . Make a million!"*

(10) Then, place another coin into your other hand and again repeat your goal command *four times:* *"Make a million! . . . Make a million! . . . Make a million! . . . Make a million!"*

(11) Continue doing this until you have transferred all of the coins from one hand to the other—each time repeating your goal command: *"Make a million!"* four times.

(12) Then transfer the coins back into your other hand, one at a time, again repeating your goal command four times with the transfer of each coin. Continue transferring the coins and repeating your goal command . . . as long as possible . . . *as frequently as possible every day.*

YOUR THOUGHTS WILL BECOME YOUR FUTURE!

Think rich . . . and you will attract money!

Chapter 62

Here's HELP! . . .

If Something Cannot Be Done . . .
Be The FIRST To Do It!

There's a foolish notion going around that there are a lot of things that cannot be done.

Yet, civilization has progressed through the ages—and the progress of mankind now is being rapidly accelerated—because the confident achievers, unperturbed by the "cannot-be-done" sceptics, deliberately continue to do the things which cannot be done.

Often, the confident achievers do not get the message that something cannot be done *until after they already have done it!*

As in the case of General Patton:

In World War II, one division of General Patton's Third Army was advancing on the enemy city of Thier.

Concerned that only *one* division was preparing to attack, Allied Supreme Headquarters sent a radio message to General Patton instructing him not to try to take the enemy stronghold at all because it would require at least *four* divisions and the cost would be extremely high.

However, by the time the message was delivered, Patton's one division already had taken Thier and he replied in typical Patton manner: "Have already taken Thier with one division. Shall I give it back?"

Remember all those dread diseases which couldn't be prevented and couldn't be cured?

I already have forgotten most of their names. So, probably, have you. Because those dread diseases which couldn't be prevented and couldn't be cured—*just don't exist anymore!*

Some scientists didn't believe that those diseases could not be prevented—so they developed vaccines which *prevented* them.

But, because some uninformed or stubborn people were not vaccinated, they were stricken with one of those incurable diseases. So scientists who did not believe that those diseases were incurable, developed a *cure* for them.

Now those diseases which could not be prevented and could not be cured—no longer exist. Many of us cannot even remember their names.

There still are diseases which cannot be prevented and cannot always be cured. But they *will* be prevented and cured by scientists who do not believe that it cannot be done.

It's an old story—like the once impossible four-minute mile which every good miler now runs in less than four minutes—so I should not devote space to it here . . .

EXCEPT for two important reasons:

(1) People *persist* in believing that things *cannot be done!* No sooner is one impossible thing accomplished, than the "cannot-be-done" sceptics (and there are millions of them!) point to the *next* impossibility.

The one really incurable disease is the "cannot-be-done" plague. It is the cause of failure of those who do not even try and of the quick-quitters whose doubts are confirmed by the first difficulty.

(2) Since there are many confident people who are immune to the "cannot-be-done" plague, *impossible things are being accomplished daily.* The rewards are instant wealth and fame.

Therefore this book of PROVEN SUCCESS METHODS would be remiss if it did not urge you *to confidently do the impossible.*

However, since the rewards for doing the impossible are instant wealth and fame, you will be competing with some superbly confident achievers—so you must be the *first* to do something which cannot be done, if you expect the big reward.

The achievers who constantly use PROVEN SUCCESS METHODS confidently do the impossible with such regularity that competition makes it necessary, not only for you to do the impossible, *but for you to be the FIRST to do it!*

Chapter 63

Here's HELP! . . .

Who Needs Other People? YOU Do!

Almost everything you have, use or need is the result of the thought and effort of others.

There are thousands, perhaps millions, of people who directly or indirectly are serving you or could serve you in some way.

Of course, you personally know only a few of the thousands—or millions—of people who have some part in providing your food, clothing, housing, furniture, automobile, job, income . . . and the list is endless.

The point is that *people are important to you.*

You can accomplish very little without the help, services and cooperation of other people.

So, throughout this book, you will find PROVEN SUCCESS METHODS for *succeeding with the people who will help you succeed.*

And, to keep you *people-conscious,* we will add a few comments here.

There are three kinds of people:

(1) The WILLS . . . *who accomplish everything!*

(2) The WON'TS . . . *who oppose and obstruct everything!*

(3) The CAN'TS . . . *who fail at everything!*

When you classify people as WILLS, WON'TS and CAN'TS (which is easy with a little practice), you know which group is *the only group which can help you succeed.*

It is only the *"WILLS . . . who accomplish everything"*—whom you should choose, contact and develop as sources, as associates and, whenever possible, as friends.

Of course, you should not ignore any person. It is better to have the goodwill of the WON'TS, than their enmity. It is charitable to encourage and help the CAN'TS.

But it is *absolutely necessary* that you secure the cooperation of the *"WILL'S, who accomplish everything"*—if you are to succeed in a BIG way!

Do you want to double your resources?

Then take the wise advice of the brilliant English clergyman, Robert Hall: "He, who has made the acquisition of a judicious and sympathizing friend may be said to have *doubled his resources.*"

It follows that by adding *another* wise and cooperative friend, you will *triple your resources.*

If you acquire a *hundred such friends,* you will pyramid your resources and increase your influence and power a *hundred times!*

Pyramiding resources and increasing influence

and power are PROVEN SUCCESS METHODS. Here's HOW: Acquire friends and associates in the "WILL" group.

The people *at the top* of every business or organization *have powerful friends* who helped them get there and who can keep them there . . . *at the top!*

Modern business and modern living are so dependent upon a *complex structure of people,* each contributing a part toward the whole of success of each other—that the "loner" is left behind in his cozy cocoon of withdrawal.

There is a saying among successful people: "The person who has no friends confirms that he has no talent, no energy, no influence, no power."

There may be the exception of a solitary artist, working alone in his cubicle—but even then, he must someday win for his masterpieces (if any), the acceptance, approval and acclamation of *many other people* if he is to achieve fame and fortune.

It has been said that the art of living is the ability to make new friends. There is much more to the art of living than that, but making new friends—especially among the "*WILLS . . . who accomplish everything*"—is a PROVEN SUCCESS METHOD which you neglect at your own risk.

Because . . . you are judged by the kind of associates and friends you have.

Way back in the 18th Century, the great German philosopher, Goethe taught: "*Tell me with whom thou art found, and I will tell thee who thou art.*"

I am sure Goethe would urge that *you be found among the "WILLS . . . who accomplish everything!"*

Chapter 64

Here's HELP! . . .

When You Are BIG, Do You Look DOWN On Others Or UP To Them?

There is a simple way to test how really BIG a person is:

(1) Does he or she look DOWN on others?

(2) Does he or she look UP to others?

That is the sure test of a person's BIGNESS.

Some people mistakenly think that being BIG enables them to look DOWN on others.

Not so! A person is only BIG when he or she looks UP to others.

People confuse BIGNESS with *physical size* as though *physical size* is the true measure of BIGNESS. *Of course it isn't!*

Physical size is the least important dimension of personal quality.

Perhaps the most revealing personal quality is *vision*—especially INNER VISION. It is with your *inner vision*—your *mental vision*—that you look DOWN on others or UP to them.

You mentally *"see"* others as people to be looked DOWN on—or UP to.

This is tremendously important to *others!* It is even more important to *you!*

Let's begin by considering why it is so tremendously important to *others* that they be looked UP to:

People—all people—have definite psychological (subconscious) needs. These needs are well known and documented. They are discussed throughout my various books because they are the keys to many PROVEN SUCCESS METHODS.

Here, in this chapter, let's consider only three psychological (subconscious) needs of *all* people which make it tremendously important to them *that they be looked UP to.*

(1) *The need to be admired.*

So, you say, that is mere vanity. Not so! Call it "vanity" if you like, but remember that *the subconscious need to be admired* is one of the most motivating and compelling of all human needs!

It surfaces from the subconscious more often in some people than in others—but the more deeply it is suppressed, the more dangerous it is if ignored.

You fulfill their *need to be admired* by looking UP to people—*all* people!

But, you say, you cannot find *anything* in *some* person which you can *look UP* to.

Find it!

No matter how insignificant you may consider a person to be—search until you find *something* about him

214

or her which you *can admire*—and then *look UP* to that person.

Always, without fail, *look UP to everybody!*

(2) *The need to be appreciated.*

Like the psychological *need to be admired*, the subconscious *need to be appreciated* is one of the most motivating and compelling of all human needs.

You *look UP* to people when you express appreciation of their accomplishments and gratitude for what they have done for you or yours.

There is *something* about *everyone* which you can find to appreciate (and compliment). *Find it!* And openly express your appreciation.

Find *something* about *everyone* to be grateful for—and openly express your gratitude.

In that way, you *look UP* to them!

(3) *The need to feel important.*

Even the most seemingly insignificant people have deep in their subconscious, the *need to feel important.*

The obviously important person fulfills his own need, but those who are not obviously important are pleading inwardly for *someone* to fulfill *their* need to feel important. You be that *someone* who finds and expresses *something* important about supposedly unimportant people.

In that way you *look UP* to them!

Well?

What's in it for *you?*

It is the difference between being LITTLE and being BIG!

Chapter 65

Here's HELP! . . .

IMAGINE . . . "As If . . ."

In the first part of this book, you learned that *your thoughts are mental pictures*.

Actually, because your thoughts are a *continuous series* of mental pictures, your thoughts are really a *mental movie*.

You are the SUPERSTAR of your mental movie. You can play the part of a failure or a success. Or you can play some kind of average or mediocre part between failure and success.

In time, you will discover that *you are actually living in real life, the part you played in your mental movie*, because the part you play in your mental movie—failure or success—*is the way you give directions to your subconscious*.

Your mental movie is your *conscious mind's* way of instructing your always receptive *subconscious*: *"This is what I want to be, have and do in real life."*

Your subconscious is *cybernetic*—which means *"goal-achieving"*, just like a guided missile. And like a guided missile, it will seek and reach whatever goal is "programed" into its guidance system.

In the case of your subconscious, its function and goal is to *materialize into the reality of your life whatever you intensely and constantly picture in your mental movie* which is the guidance director of your subconscious.

Your subconscious is your channel to *Infinite Power* and therefore can *attract to you* or *guide you to WHATEVER is necessary*—the education, training, opportunities, financing, personal contacts—*to enable you to attain your life-goal.*

The power of your subconscious to influence or actually arrange the circumstances and events which *materialize your intense, constant mental pictures into reality* is miraculous beyond human comprehension.

But we *do* know that *this is so* and that the *Bible* is stating a proven scientific fact: *"As a man THINKETH, so IS he."*

This is the teaching of *all* religions throughout the centuries. It is the profound conclusion of philosophy. It is proven again and again by psychology, psychiatry and behavioral science . . .

"As a man THINKETH, so IS he."

Or . . . *"so he will become"*, because man is destined to become the reality of his mental pictures.

All of this is documented in the first part of this book and you may review it there and in my other books.

It is reviewed briefly at the beginning of this

217

chapter so that you will be mentally prepared for the PROVEN SUCCESS METHOD of "*As If*".

The miraculous psychological power of "*As If*" has been known in some degree by all of the GREAT THINKERS since the beginning of reasoning thought.

But it was the great psychologist, William James, of Harvard, who turned the spotlight of his brilliant mind on the psychological method of "*As If*" and illuminated its *unlimited possibilities in personal goal-achievement.*

Your effective use of the PROVEN SUCCESS METHOD of "*As If*" will:

(1) Enable you to become *the kind of person you want to be*

(2) Attain any *life-goal* you desire

(3) Get WHATEVER you *want* in life

There are three easy-to-understand, easy-to-use steps in the PROVEN SUCCESS METHOD which psychologists call "*As If*".

The first step is: IMAGINE "*As If* . . ."

By doing this you actually IMAGINE *your future into reality!*

IMAGINE (*mentally picture*) the kind of person you want to become.

Psychologists call this "*constantly visualizing a mental picture of your ideal self-image.*

This mental picture of your IDEAL YOU must be a *mental movie* of your looking, talking, acting and doing everything "*As If*" *you already have become the kind of person you want to be.*

In your IMAGINATION, you must *clearly and*

intensely "see" yourself—exactly, in as much detail as possible—*"As If" you already have become your IDEAL YOU.*

In your IMAGINATION, you must vividly *"live"* your future *as you want it to be.*

If you do this *intensely . . . continuously,* in every moment you can spare from your necessary daily activities . . . day after day . . . week after week . . . month after month . . . *YOU ACTUALLY WILL BECOME the kind of person you want to be!*

It will seem like a miracle!

But it will not be a miracle; it simply will be a known psychological method, a proven scientific procedure.

If you prefer to view it in terms of religion— your mental picture was your prayer, and the answer to your prayer was prophesied in the Bible: *"As a man THINKETH, so IS he."*

If you prefer to view your becoming what you mentally picture—in terms of philosophy, we can go all the way back to the great philosopher of ancient Rome, Marcus Aurelius, who wrote: *"Our LIFE is what our THOUGHTS make it."*

Or in terms of modern logic and the *Law of Consistency: "ACTION (in this case, BECOMING) must be consistent with constant THOUGHT."*

Or, in terms of psychology and William James: *"Belief (constant thought expressed through mental pictures) CREATES THE ACTUAL FACT."*

Having learned to IMAGINE "As If . . ."

Now learn to THINK "As If . . ."

In the next chapter . . .

Chapter 66

Here's HELP! . . .

THINK . . . "As If . . ."

The preceding chapter explained the first step in the miraculous power of the psychological method of "As If", which was taught so brilliantly by psychologist William James of Harvard.

This first step, as explained in the preceding chapter was: IMAGINE . . . "As If." By using your IMAGINATION, you can mentally "see" yourself as the kind of person you want to become. You are the SUPERSTAR of your own *mental movie* and, in your IMAGINATION, you *become* the kind of person you want to be.

Then, by intensely and constantly IMAGINING yourself "As If" you *already have become* the kind of person you want to be, you set in motion subconscious forces which, as psychologist William James taught, "CREATE THE ACTUAL FACT."

So now we come to the second step in using the miraculous power of the psychological method of "As If".

This second step is to THINK . . . "*As If*".

To THINK . . . "*As If*" . . . is a more advanced and powerful psychological method than the beginning first step of IMAGINING mental pictures of the kind of person you want to become.

When you THINK . . . "*As If*", you *activate the mental pictures into reality* through the *power of positive thinking*.

You follow the advice of the world-famous preacher-psychologist-writer, Dr. Norman Vincent Peale, the leading exponent of the *power of positive thinking*, who taught: "THINK *success*, VISUALIZE *success*, and you will set in motion the power force of the realizable wish. When the *mental picture* or attitude is strongly enough held, it actually seems to *control conditions and circumstances.*"

It does, indeed!

A mental picture strongly enough held does control conditions and circumstances!

And when, as Dr. Peale taught, you THINK success, VISUALIZE success—*you do set in motion the power force of the realizable wish!*

And as psychologist William James taught, you must THINK "*As If*" you *are* successful.

When you THINK "*As If*" you *are* successful, you rapidly acquire that *all-important, all-powerful* SUCCESS ATTITUDE!

As Dr. Walter Scott, famous psychologist and president of Northwestern University, taught: "*Success or failure in business is caused more by MENTAL ATTITUDES than by mental capacities.*

221

So you *must* constantly maintain a SUCCESS ATTITUDE . . . beginning NOW!

You must THINK "*As If*" you *are* successful.

One example:

If you want to be RICH . . . you must constantly THINK RICH!

You must constantly mentally picture your *being* RICH! You must *constantly visualize* in your IMAGINATION the *abundance of great wealth*—the fine possessions, the important and rewarding activities, and the bountiful services you would render others.

You must THINK RICH!

You must become *money-conscious,* use the "Dollar Bill Book Mark" (described in a previous chapter), impress into your subconscious *thousands of times* the forceful *goal-command:* MAKE A MILLION! (also described in a previous chapter.)

To *be* RICH, you must THINK RICH!

You can use that same method to get WHATEVER you want in life . . . *happiness* . . . *popularity* . . . *power* . . . *fame* . . . *WHATEVER YOU WANT!*

Then you will be using the second step in the miraculously powerful psychological method: "*As If*" . . .

THINK "*As If*". . . .

Now for the third and final step: ACT "*As If*". . . .

In the next chapter . . .

Chapter 67

Here's HELP! . . .

ACT . . . "As If . . ."

The two preceding chapters explained the first two of the three steps in the miraculous psychological method of "*As If*".

(1) IMAGINE . . . "*As If*"

(2) THINK . . . "*As If*"

Now we shall explain the third method which is even more psychologically powerful:

(3) ACT . . . "As If"

This is the basis of William James' teaching of the miraculous power of "*As If.*"

So, I shall quote the great psychologist directly:

"Action seems to follow feeling, but really action and feeling go together; and *by regulating the ACTION*, which is under the more direct control of the will, *we can indirectly regulate the FEELING*, which is not."

Thus, psychologist William James teaches us

that by ACTING "*As If*" we feel better, or we feel happy, or we feel confident, or we feel courageous—*we actually cause ourselves to FEEL the way we ACT!*

William James expresses it this way: "Thus, the sovereign voluntary path to cheerfulness, if your cheerfulness be lost, is to sit up cheerfully and to *ACT* and speak *AS IF* cheerfulness *were already there.*"

So you have it in the great psychologist's own words that by ACTING "*As If*" we *already* feel the way we want to feel: "*we can indirectly regulate the feeling.*" By consciously controlling action, we control feeling.

People used to believe *only* that *action followed feeling.* So if you *felt* unhappy, you *acted* unhappy. Your *feeling* unhappy *caused* you to *act* unhappy.

Of course this remains true.

However, William James announced a new and miraculously helpful psychological concept:

Not only does *action follow feeling*—but *feeling follows action.*

So, if you *feel unhappy*, you can ACT "*As If*" you *are cheerful* and thus *change your feeling of unhappiness to a feeling of cheerfulness*—to be *consistent* with your ACTING "*As If*" you are cheerful.

So, again, we see the *Law of Consistency* at work.

When you ACT "*As If*" (however you *want* to *feel*), then—*to be consistent*—you will *feel* the way you *act.*

This PROVEN SUCCESS METHOD enables you to *change* and *control* your feelings, your emotions, your mind-moods—simply by ACTING "*As If*".

A few brief examples:

224

ACT *"As If"* you *are* cheerful . . . and you will *feel* cheerful.

ACT *"As If"* you *are* confident . . . and you will *feel* confident.

ACT *"As If"* you *are* enthusiastic . . . and you will *feel* enthusiastic.

ACT *"As If"* you *are* friendly . . . and you will *feel* friendly.

If someone offends you and you begin to feel resentful and angry—*change* those self-damaging feelings by ACTING *"As If" you are unperturbed by and tolerant of rude people*—and instantly your feelings will *change* from resentment and anger to unperturbed tolerance.

Thus, you can *"turn off"* undesirable and self-damaging feelings.

Examples could be continued endlessly, but the preceding examples are sufficient to illustrate this very useful PROVEN SUCCESS METHOD *which enables you to change and control your feelings, emotions and mind-moods*—simply by ACTING *"As If"*.

You now have at your command a psychological technique which can work "miracles" in your life! Be sure to use *all three methods:*

(1) IMAGINE . . . *"As If* . . ."
(2) THINK . . . *"As If* . . ."
(3) ACT . . . *"As If* . . ."

Then, *whatever* you IMAGINE *"As If"* . . . THINK *"As If"* . . . ACT *"As If"* . . . will actually become a reality because your imagination, thoughts and actions are *goal commands* to your subconscious which will direct you to or attract to you *whatever is consistent* with your dominant thoughts and actions.

Chapter 68

Here's HELP! . . .

How To Develop And Use
"Triggered" Automatic Responses

Life is, to a large extent, routine.

Even the most unusual, exciting and varied lives still retain the basic elements of routine.

In the lives of most of us, the same *kind* of experiences, events and conditions reoccur with frequent regularity. *Repetitive situations.*

Psychologists and success counselors have found that every person is more effective and successful if he or she develops and uses *automatic responses* which are *"triggered"* by repetitive situations—*thus capitalizing on routine.*

Instead of going into a long and complex psychological and behavioral explanation of the desirability of *"triggered" automatic responses,* this PROVEN SUCCESS METHOD is more easily learned through typical examples.

For example, when you are *criticized* (you think, unjustly), instead of replying with a heated rebuttal, precipitating an argument with increased ill feelings—you should have a *proven-effective, ready* reply.

You should use this *same* reply—*automatically* —*whenever* you are *criticized*. This is what is known as a "*triggered*" automatic response because *any* criticism "triggers" it (sets it off) spontaneously and automatically.

You may compose your own "*triggered*" *automatic response to all criticism,* but the following response has been proven highly effective (for many psychological reasons) so it is suggested that you use it until you compose one which you find more effective.

Example—when you are *criticized*—you respond pleasantly and tolerantly: "I understand *how* you feel and I understand *why* you feel as you do."

Important: Do not say more. Stop right there. Do not launch a rebuttal. Do not argue. Do not discuss the criticism further. Give the impression of finality. You have acknowledged the criticism and stated forthrightly that *you understand* not only *how* the criticizer feels, but *why* he or she feels that way.

No further response is *required* of you—and *you should offer none.*

You have cleverly left your criticizer "high and dry"—conversationally stranded. *You have not admitted that your criticizer was right*—nor have you argued (unproductively) that he or she was wrong.

You have been tolerant and sympathetic— *without agreeing with the criticism.* You merely stated that you *understood* "how" and "why" the person criticized you.

And you did so with *finality*, making it obvious that as far as you were concerned, that *concluded* the matter. PERIOD.

If possible, procede with an entirely different topic of conversation. If this is not possible, simply remain silent. If your criticizer continues the criticism, just *repeat your same response* and do not discuss the criticism further.

Now—STOP here and thoughtfully review this chapter to this point. You will see what is meant by a *"triggered" automatic response.*

(1) You prepare in advance for such situations as are likely to occur—in this example: *criticism*—so that you have ready a *prepared, automatic response* which already has been proven *psychologically effective.*

(2) Your use of this *same* response *always* is "*triggered*" (put into instant effect) by the *same kind* of situation—in this example: *criticism of you by another.*

(3) Having made your response, *calmly* and *pleasantly,* you indicate by your tone and attitude that your response is your *final* statement on the matter. If the other person persists, *simply repeat your response* with the attitude that the other person must not have understood that your statement was as far as you were going to procede in discussing that subject.

Now let's consider a somewhat similar example: *stopping an argument* before it gets heated.

It is assumed that you have the good sense *not to start an argument, yourself.*

So, when another person starts an argument with you, it should "*trigger*" the following good-natured, tolerant *automatic response* from you: "*You* certainly have as much right to *your opinion* as I have to mine—and *you may very well be right.*"

Stop there. You previously had stated your opinion. The other person disagreed and began to argue.

You stopped the argument with a *"triggered" automatic response* which made apparently forthright "concessions" (which actually existed anyway) by stating:

(1) The other person *certainly* had *as much right to his or her opinion*—as you had to yours.

Note that you did not concede any substance of the argument, itself. You merely *conceded* the other person's *right* to his or her *opinion.*

(2) You made it equally clear that *you also* had the *same right* to *your* opinion (which is a fair and acceptable statement).

(3) You also *conceded* that the other person *could* be right. (You *did not concede* that it was probable, reasonable, *or even worth arguing about*—only that it was *"possible".*)

(4) Your statement had the finality of making it clear *that having made those fair and forthright "concessions", you did not propose to engage in an argument.* PERIOD.

Now, to demonstrate the wide-range of possibilities in effectively using the *"triggered" automatic response,* here are several examples of its use in very different circumstances.

For example, *always before talking over the telephone:*

(1) The *"trigger"* is your picking up the telephone (to answer a call or to make one).

229

(2) Your *automatic response* to this *"trigger"* is that *you remind yourself:* "I shall express *gratitude, goodwill* and *good wishes."*

This is the 3-G PROVEN SUCCESS METHOD described in a previous chapter, so I shall not repeat it here.

The point is that you can use *any* object or situation to *"trigger"* your *automatic response* which you have learned *in advance* and which is *psychologically effective.*

Remember, that the *same* object or situation *must always "trigger" the same automatic response.*

Finally, let us consider how this method can be used to *alleviate* the *constant or frequent heartbreak of excessive grief.*

This is not to minimize the personal tragedy of the loss of one you love. No one can do that.

It is, as stated here, a method to alleviate the *constant or frequent heartbreak of excessive grief.*

There are many psycho-emotional causes for *excessive grief,* but we shall not discuss them here, except to state that *many people use excessive grief, itself, as an automatic response to a variety of "triggers" which they frequently see or recall.*

Those unfortunate people who *mentally and emotionally re-live personal tragedy* as a response to seeing a photograph or some object which reminds them of a departed loved one—can use those same "reminder objects" as "triggers" for the following *more loving benediction.*

Excessive grief which results from mentally

and emotionally re-living scenes and emotions related to a departed loved one—can be lovingly and reverently replaced by the intensely-thought benediction: *"I love you! . . . I love you! . . . I love you!"*

No excessive grief, no heartbreak, no recall of tragic memories. *Substitute healing love . . .* "*I love you! . . . I love you! . . . I love you!*" . . . repeated mentally until *love replaces heartbreak,* as it always will.

Then focus your thoughts on something else.

Whenever a photograph or other object "triggers" memories of a departed loved one, let your response be *not grief, but love.* And confine your *"triggered"* response to be just three all-encompassing words: *"I love you! . . . I love you! . . . I love you!"*

DO NOT use *other* word-thought which will renew your grief, such as: "I *miss* you!" . . . "I *need* you!" . . . "*I cannot stand being without you!*" Such heartbreaking word-thoughts are *needlessly self-punishing.*

Let the word-thought: *"I love you! . . . I love you! . . . I love you!"* . . . replace all painful memories and grief-recall.

Let love take over completely. Love is the only adequate and healing response.

Chapter 69

Here's HELP! . . .

Whatever Happens: There Are Only Five Things You Can Do

Because WHATEVER happens to you, *there are only five things you can do,* it obviously is desirable that you thoroughly understand each of these five alternates.

You usually can *choose* which of the five kinds of response will be most successful.

The choice is yours. Therefore, so is the responsibility.

By studying the five possible kinds of response to *whatever* may happen to you in the future, *you will be prepared to respond successfully to each happening as it occurs.*

Here are the five kinds of responses you can use *whatever* happens:

(1) *OVER-response*

(2) *UNDER-response*

(3) *DELAYED-response*

(4) *NON-response*

(5) *OPPOSITE-response*

Depending upon the happening, your choice of response should vary. Each kind of response can be used successfully and each can be disastrous—depending upon your ability to choose the most effective response to use on each different occasion and your skill in using it.

Because you *must* use one of the five kinds of responses to *everything* which happens to you *all day, every day*—your need to understand all five responses and how to use them effectively—is vitally important to your success in life.

Therefore, we shall devote the next five chapters—each to one of the five different responses. You will learn *why, when* and *how* to use each response—and, equally important, *when not to use each response.*

Chapter 70

Here's HELP! . . .

Why, When And How You Should Or Should Not OVER-Respond

You *must* respond, in one of five ways, to *everything* which happens to you—*all day, every day.*

Which way you choose to respond—and how successfully you respond—will greatly affect your success in life.

Even if you choose *not to respond at all,* you are using a *deliberate* kind of response—known, psychologically as *"NON-response"*—which is a very useful way to respond to many situations, as you will learn in a later chapter in this series of five chapters, each teaching a different kind of response.

This chapter concerns *OVER-response.*

OVER-response is best described by some examples. Here are several:

Someone says something which angers you and you *OVER-respond* by physically or verbally attacking with furious violence. *Such OVER-response with violence makes you a sure loser!*

You either lose on the spot by receiving a physical or verbal beating—or if you "win" (and you cannot *really* "win"), you set yourself up for *future retaliation* by the enemy you certainly will have made. *Your enemy has all of the options,* including the time to strike back—physically, with weapons, or lawsuits, or damaging rumors, or harm to your family, home or business, or with any of a wide range of damaging alternatives *against which you can prepare no defense* because of the countless forms of damaging retaliation and your uncertainty concerning *when* your enemy will strike back.

You only can be certain that some day, somehow, somewhere, *your enemy will retaliate.* So you live in apprehension and anxiety—awaiting the consequences of your *OVER-response in anger and violence.*

So never—whatever the provocation—never *OVER-respond in anger by physically or verbally attacking with furious violence.*

The opposite also is true. Instead of attack—it is a form of retreat.

Never OVER-respond in fear, anxiety or panic.

People are afraid of so many things that it would not be practical to try to list each "fear situation" and the reasons why *OVER-response in fear, anxiety or panic is never a solution; it greatly intensifies the problem.*

Fear and anxiety solve absolutely nothing. They increase the difficulties and impede the solution.

Another common and self-defeating form of *OVER-response* is *"over-acting" as a form of ego-inflation.*

Thus, although a situation requires conciliation and logical negotiation, *some* self-inflating minority leaders, *some* labor leaders, *most* militant activists, and *all* demagogues threaten: *"WE DEMAND!!!"* The more stupid add: "And *our demands are non-negotiable!!!"*

Of course, this *OVER-response by "over-acting" with demands and threats* is merely to impress *their own egos and their followers*—because it impresses intelligent negotiators not at all. And it is offensive and insulting to the general public which sees and hears it in the news media.

Another self-damaging form of *OVER-response* is the *"you, too!!!"* criticism-response. This way to make a bad situation worse is to *OVER-respond* to criticism by retorting, "How dare *you* criticize *me,* when *you* did (*criticism*) . . . and (*criticism*) . . . and (*criticism*)!!!" And so, criticism begets criticism in an escalating spiral. It is an *OVER-response* which solves nothing, helps nobody, and creates resentment . . . *fast!*

Then, there is the similar *OVER-response* by *"name-calling"*—either belligerently aloud or secretly in the privacy of one's thoughts (where it teaches an evil lesson to the subconscious!).

Someone says something which offends you, or which you merely don't like, or with which you disagree. It may be said in person, or in a speech, or over television or radio. Or you may disagree or resent something the other person has written.

If you *OVER-respond by calling the speaker or writer one or a series of derogatory names* as a childish means of expressing disagreement and displeasure—*you are a sure loser!*

If you call a person a derogatory name to his face, *he will never forget it!* Being called a derogatory name is an insult *which makes an instant and lasting impression in the subconscious.* It incurs lasting resentment which cannot be entirely erased either by apology or making amends. Lesson: *Do not do it in the first place!*

Much more prevalent is *"silent name-calling"* in which a person inwardly expresses disagreement with and dislike of another by *"silent name-calling"* in the privacy of his thoughts. Many people get a *temporary* emotional release from *"silent name-calling"*—but it teaches a permanently self-damaging *OVER-response* to their subconscious which will increasingly repeat the method.

We could continue to list the penalties of *OVER-response* for the remainder of this book. But we shall stop here, hoping that the preceding examples are sufficient.

What can we say *good* about *OVER-response?*

Very little! *OVER-response* can be used to emphasize and exaggerate one's opinion of a happening—but usually it is contrived *"play-acting."* Unless expertly performed, it sounds and looks as phoney as it is.

The *Oooohers* and *Ahhhers* who are pretenders of culture at art exhibits and concerts are evidence enough that *OVER-response* exaggerates poor *"play-acting"* more than the impression it intends to create.

We shall leave it there and get on with the more rewarding PROVEN SUCCESS METHOD of *UNDER-response.*

In the next chapter . . .

Chapter 71

Here's HELP! ...

Relax...In The Benefits Of UNDER-Response!

In the previous chapter, we considered the disadvantages—ranging from ill will to disaster—incurred by those who *OVER-respond* to what happens to them.

Now, we shall consider *UNDER-response*—which is the opposite reaction to *OVER-response*. Being the opposite reaction, we should expect opposite and therefore, generally better results from *UNDER-response*. And this is true.

It is the difference between going through life with an over-heated, knocking engine (which inevitably will blow a vital part), and going smoothly through life with cool, calm control.

UNDER-response does not take life and its irritable people and annoying circumstances *too seriously*.

It is not getting *uptight!*

UNDER-response is taking Kipling's advice:

"Meet with *triumph* and *disaster* and treat those two *imposters* just the same."

In fact, Kipling's entire poem "If" is a masterpiece of teaching *UNDER-response*. It not only is "recommended reading", it is *"required memorizing"* for anyone who would live calmly, sensibly and *successfully* in this complex and often unpredictably tragic world.

UNDER-response is "not burning down the barn to kill the rats" because rats are simply not deserving of our overly destructive *OVER-response*—and neither are other pests: animal, insect or human.

One of the many advantages of *UNDER-response* is that you retain the option to apply increasing pressure later, if needed. And, by *degrees,* only to the extent needed.

UNDER-response gives you *control.* And with *control,* you have power and leadership.

It is a PROVEN SUCCESS METHOD worth your learning and using.

As is *DELAYED-response,* described in the next chapter . . .

Chapter 72

Here's HELP! . . .

Do Not React Rashly! Become A Master Of DELAYED-Response!

Throughout all of my books of PROVEN SUCCESS METHODS you will find frequent recommendations of *patience-power*.

The reason is that during forty years of research and testing of success methods, I have found that *best results are obtained by first considering all possible alternatives,* then choosing a course of action clearly charted by *all the facts.*

Throughout your entire life, you will be confronted by very few emergencies which require *instant* action.

But every day you will make decisions in which a *DELAYED-response* will give you time to first consider *all possible alternatives* before committing yourself.

This is not an advocacy of procrastination.

It is an advocacy of reaching decisions as rap-

*idly as consideration of all possible alternatives permits—
then acting rapidly, with confidence.*

The time usually required to consider alternatives may be a matter of *seconds* or *minutes*. It is *not* suggested that a *DELAYED-response* be a slow, ponderous, time-wasting procedure. Indeed, it saves time because *it is faster to do a thing right—than to do it over!* Assuming that there is even the opportunity to do it over!

Of course, there are important and complex decisions which involve many alternatives and detailed analysis—including your seeking expert advice. These do require time. So be it. Do not permit yourself to be rushed into rash, hasty, reckless action.

And view with deep suspicion, anybody who is so eager for your favorable response that he will not permit you time to consider alternatives—*and consequences!*

If you wish to build a reputation for—*and a fortune as the result of—*making successful decisions, become a master of the *DELAYED-response.*

And do not underestimate the power of *NON-response.*

Described in the next chapter . . .

Chapter 73

Here's HELP! . . .

NON-Response—The Art Of Doing Nothing . . . Successfully!

There are many times when the most effective response, the most successful response—is *NO response at all!*

In my book, *Thoughts To Build On,* is a chapter titled: "The Gentle Art of Letting Alone".

Among other things, that chapter states that "in most cases—*all avoidable*—*we initiate our own troubles* by two actions: (1) Unnecessary involvement or, much worse, *over*-involvement, and (2) Unnecessary reaction or, much worse, *over*-reaction".

And then the chapter proceeds to teach the "Gentle Art Of Letting Alone". It is an art well worth your learning.

Also, in my book, *Thoughts To Build On,* is a chapter titled "Let It Rain" which is based on the great wisdom of a simple, little statement by Longfellow: *"For after all, the best thing one can do when it is raining, is to let it rain."*

And so we should—because we must. There are many situations in life about which, like the rain, we can do nothing.

It does us no good to respond to them by being irritated, annoyed, worried—or to respond in *any* way. The only appropriate response is *NON-response.*

However, there are many situations—often daily—when you are confronted with making a choice. There often are many alternatives.

A PROVEN SUCCESS METHOD is: *Always include in your list of alternative choices—the consideration of NON-response.*

It is not necessary that you do something—*anything!*—just because someone asks you to.

Remember that one of the choices available to you is *NON-response*—you can deliberately choose *not* to do it. *You can let it alone!*

Just last night, I heard a speech by a leading psychiatrist who said that one of the principal problems of his emotionally upset patients is their feeling that they *must* do certain things; that they are *required* to do things *because someone (almost anyone) expects them to.*

The psychiatrist said that when he convinced these patients that they have a clear *freedom of choice,* and that one alternative is *NON-response—not doing anything* —then the patients are released from their feelings of being controlled, compelled, manipulated. And are cured.

This confirms what I have written in my other books and the point I want to emphasize in this chapter.

You must not develop a *"puppet complex"*. You must be constantly aware of *your* alternative of *NON-response*.

In fact, you should *practice NON-response* to reinforce its existence as an alternative which *you control*.

Practice what psychiatrists recommend as: *"Let the telephone ring."*

Rushing to answer a ringing telephone is an established behavioral pattern of almost everybody. So establish firmly in your own mind that whether or *not* you will answer your ringing telephone is a matter of *your own choosing* . . . that you do not *have* to answer it . . . that *if* you do so, it will be entirely *voluntary*.

So let your telephone ring occasionally.

Or, at least, let it ring until you *consciously and deliberately decide* whether or *not* you *will* answer it.

This may be a little rude, because you will be wasting a few seconds of someone else's time—but it will keep you from being like Pavlov's dogs who were trained to slobber at the ringing of a bell!

Now, the purpose of teaching the alternative of *NON-response* is *not* to make you stubborn, obstinate or negative. It simply is to give you the feeling of *deliberate and thoughtful control of your own acts*.

It is *not* necessary that you join every conflict, take sides in every cause (especially controversial causes) and thus gain an additional supply of enemies. Yes, admittedly, you may also gain some friends, but the enemies made in controversy seem to remain long after the friends have faded into acquaintances. Anyway, there are many quicker, easier, better ways to make friends; but there are few quicker, easier ways to make enemies.

Over-involvement in too many causes diffuses your time, dissipates your energies and disorganizes your life.

You do not have to accept every task, shoulder every burden, assume every responsibility which may be offered or thrust upon you.

Nobody made you General Manager of the Universe, and you do not have to take upon yourself the responsibilities of personally solving many, if any, of its vast problems.

Nor are you required to worry about how others, who have been elected, selected, or profitably employed precisely for such purpose, manage situations which only remotely affect you, if at all. Or about which you really can do very little, if anything.

Certainly you do not have to plunge physically, emotionally or mentally into every crisis which does not involve you. And I can assure you that the people actually involved in those crises are not the least concerned about *your own* personal problems.

Of course, as a citizen of the world, you should keep informed and be interested. Beyond that point of citizen interest, you should be consciously aware of the various kinds of response available for further involvement.

And not the least of these is *NON-response— the art of doing nothing . . . successfully!*

Chapter 74

Here's HELP! . . .

OPPOSITE-Response—The Art Of Doing The Unexpected . . . Surprisingly!

The *OPPOSITE-response* can be used in almost any situation but it is most effective in handling a potentially unpleasant situation.

It is best explained by examples:

When something or someone irritates you, the *expected response* would be for you to become *angry*.

The *OPPOSITE-response* is for you to *laugh!*

And . . . you will happily discover that the *OPPOSITE-response* of *laughter* is a much more effective response than anger. Instead of anger escalating into hostility, laughter will relieve the tension—provided that the laughter is not insultingly provocative, but demonstrates unoffended good humor.

There is an old, a true, and a very wise saying:

"Laughter is your declaration of superiority over whatever befalls you."

And another: *"When you must either curse or laugh—choose to laugh."*

The inconveniences and annoyances of life should be accepted, not with an ill-tempered response of irritability, but with the *OPPOSITE-response of good humor.*

As Lincoln said, "A man is as happy as he makes up his mind to be." If you make up your mind to be happy, you must make up your mind to respond to unpleasantness with the *OPPOSITE-response* of pleasantness. Otherwise, you will not be happy. Nor will those around you. Like happiness, unhappiness is contagious.

The *OPPOSITE-response*, instead of complaining, is to compliment. Did you know that *you can express a complaint in the form of a sincere compliment?* You can! Think about it.

The *OPPOSITE-response* to rudeness is to express sympathetic understanding (reinforced by genuine goodwill).

The *OPPOSITE-response* to criticism is not the expected response of resentment, but honest words of appreciation for the constructive advice contained in the criticism.

The *OPPOSITE-response* in dealing with an adversary is to do him or her a favor—not with the attitude of trying to "buy goodwill"—but with gracious friendliness, "no-strings-attached".

The *OPPOSITE-response* to learning that someone is "talking behind your back" *unfavorably*—is to frequently talk about that person "behind his or her back" *favorably*. It is amazing how fast that news will get to the other person! And result in an instant change in attitude!

The preceding examples of the unexpected *OPPOSITE-response* should be sufficient, not only to explain it, but to encourage you to *use it at every opportunity*.

You *must* respond to *every* happening in your life with *one of the five responses* described in this and the preceding chapters.

Your happiness and success in life will be greatly influenced by which response you choose and how effectively you use it.

Every minute devoted to studying these chapters will be pure gold!

Chapter 75

Here's HELP! . . .

How To Be HELPED—Not HURT— By Criticism

There is a chapter in this book advising *you not to criticize others,* and teaching more pleasant and more effective psychological methods to accomplish the results you would intend your criticism to produce.

Hopefully, *you* will use more effective psychological methods than direct criticism, but you may expect *others to criticize you.*

Therefore, it is necessary to learn how to be *helped*—not *hurt*—by criticism.

Let us start by eliminating the *"hurt"*.

Most of the *"hurts"* of criticism merely are *hurt feelings* resulting from ego damage.

Because your "feelings" are emotional, the way to eliminate your "hurt feelings" (emotions) simply is *not to take criticism emotionally.* Do not inflict upon yourself the damage of being resentful or angry.

249

If criticism deflates your ego, it shows that your ego needs toughening—or that the criticism is deserved (even if ineptly delivered).

So much for generalities; let's get to specifics.

Criticism is the result of one or a combination of three things:

(1) The person criticizing you merely is giving vent to his pent-up emotions: envy, resentment, anger, fear, among others.

Just ignore it. Such criticism is a usual form of what psychiatrists call "catharsis". You are, perhaps unwillingly, a psychotherapist helping the "patient" rid his system of self-damaging emotions. Count it your good deed for the day—then ignore it.

There is some psychological significance in the fact that *you* were selected as the target—but just ignore it and forget it. It isn't worth psychoanalysis.

(2) The person criticizing you may be trying to build himself up by tearing you down. Or, he may, for some reason, simply be trying to tear you down. Or, he may use criticism just to appear important and formidable, at no expense.

Beware of the person who accompanies his criticism with such remarks as: "This is only for *your* own good." (Nonsense! It is for *his* ego-satisfaction!) Or the person who says: "I am criticizing you only because I *love you.*" (Oh yeah? Then why *hurt* you? There are less painful ways of helping, guiding and teaching those one loves. Or even doesn't love.)

The person who criticizes you for the purpose of tearing you down (for *any* reason) proves himself an adversary—and should be regarded as such. He is like a sword-fish which uses its mouth as a weapon.

Nevertheless, the criticism of an enemy may be more frank, more pointed *and more correct* than the criticism (or "helpful suggestion") of a friend—or even your own self-criticism.

Rochefoucauld wrote, *"The opinions of our enemies come nearer to the truth about us than do our own opinions."* Our enemies are looking for our faults more intently than we. Ignore your enemy, but never his criticism of you.

When an adversary or enemy criticizes you:

(a) First, rid his criticism of all emotion—his and yours.

(b) Then, judge the criticism logically, impartially—solely on its merits—for it may reveal needed corrections which your friends hesitate to mention.

You can learn much of value from the criticism of an adversary or enemy—*if you do not let your judgment be distorted by your emotions of resentment and anger.*

(3) Criticism may be good advice—without the sugar-coating.

Do not refuse criticism because it is distasteful to you. *Do not refuse good advice because it comes in the form of criticism.* As I look back on a long and eventful life, I find that, because I resented criticism, I ignored the valuable advice and information it contained. I now consider this to have been one of my most costly faults. It cost me several fortunes and countless friends.

In fact, criticism is so valuable, you should *ask* for it!

If you are not getting the results you think you should, begin re-checking the situation by *critically* examining *your* part in it. Do not rely on your own judgment because you may be rationalizing your failure. Instead, ask others—the ones who should know—what is wrong and especially what *you* are doing wrong.

Many an insecure employee has saved his job by the sensible procedure of frankly asking his employer what he was doing wrong, how he could correct it, how he could do his job better and how he could make himself more valuable to his company. Employers do not fire employees like that. They *promote* them!

So . . . do not be like the timid person who said that he would rather be ruined by praise than saved by criticism.

Most criticism is helpful if you eliminate the emotions of both the giver and receiver.

The emotional factor—and sometimes the destructive intent—may make being criticized an unpleasant experience.

Surgery also is an unpleasant experience, but it can be very beneficial—and necessary. *Like surgery, criticism can remove the source of trouble—and the cut will heal.*

So don't criticize criticism.

Chapter 76

Here's HELP! . . .

Be UNDERWHELMED! Do Not Make A "Big Thing" Out Of ANY Happening!

In *A Psalm of Life,* Longfellow exclaimed, "Life is real! Life is earnest!" To which a stoic added, "But you don't have to get red in the neck about it."

Personally, I like the evenhandedness of Kipling's: "Meet with triumph and disaster, and treat those two *imposters* just the same."

Perhaps, you will get "more" out of life by over-emphasizing and over-emotionalizing the passing events. In that way, you will get more elation . . . and more heartbreak. That may not be the best choice—physically, mentally, emotionally.

You have an alternative.

You can choose to be UNDERWHELMED.

That means that you will not over-emphasize,

over-emotionalize, over-dramatize the passing events which constitute your life.

Instead of being *overwhelmed* by the thrill—or the calamity—of passing events, you are UNDERWHELMED.

You do not emphasize each success as a great *triumph*. You accept success as a *happening*. You are pleased, but you are UNDERWHELMED. You do not make a "big thing" out of it. And you resolve to do better.

You do not emphasize failure as a great *disaster*. You accept failure for what it is—a *happening* on your road to your goal. And it is no more than that. So you do not make a "big thing" out of it. You are UNDERWHELMED. And you resolve to do better.

Think of the events of your life as you think of the events of nature. It rains. So it is raining. That's all. It is raining. And the rain will stop. But, meanwhile, it is raining. No "big thing". You are UNDERWHELMED.

Or, the sun is shining. No cause to jump for joy. No "big thing". The sun often shines. You are UNDERWHELMED. Because some day it will rain. Then the sun will shine again.

But . . . there *is* tragedy. It is very real. And it *hurts*. Of course, it *hurts!* But it will hurt less if you *accept* it. Do as William James advises, "Be willing to have it so. *Acceptance of what has happened is the first step to overcoming the consequences of any misfortune.*"

As I wrote in my book, *Thoughts To Build On:* "By acceptance you attain a spiritual transition from sorrow to tranquility." That is better than being overwhelmed. And it turns that page in the *Book of Life* to the next page which reads: *"When Fate closes one door, Faith opens another. Seek the open door."*

But the events of life seldom are really great tragedies.

Or, great disasters.

Or, great triumphs.

They simply are *"happenings".*

And you should avoid letting *"happenings"* reach *"triumph"* or *"disaster"* levels in your thoughts and feelings.

If events, instead of being *"happenings"* are over-emotionalized into being *"big things"*—*triumphs* and *disasters*—then your life will be a wild roller-coaster ride of emotional ups and downs . . . and you will become an unstable person.

It is better to accept the happenings of life with the equanimity with which you accept the happenings of sunshine and rain.

And be serenely UNDERWHELMED.

Chapter 77

Here's HELP! . . .

Ridicule The Negatives Out Of Your Life!

The use of ridicule has been much slandered.
Indeed, ridicule is a dangerous weapon. It has been called *"a blade without a hilt"* because it wounds the user as much as the intended victim.

But I have noticed that ridicule is criticized because—*and ONLY*—when it is used to undermine that which is *good*.

So I want to recommend the psychological method of using ridicule against that which is *bad*.

Specifically, I want to urge you to *ridicule the negatives out of your life!*

You do this by using what psychologists call "affirmations", which simply are *intensely thought* (or written, for extra emphasis) *statements of positive belief*.

This method can most simply be taught by examples, some of which you may be able to use or adapt yourself, and you can easily compose specific affirmations *ridiculing the negatives* out of your own life.

Here are some general examples:

(1) "It would be *ridiculous* to worry about what *might* happen in the future—because *anything* might happen!"

(2) "It would be *ridiculous* to devote even one second to *worrying about the past*—because the past is gone forever and cannot be changed."

(3) "It would be *ridiculous* ever to *criticize anybody*—because criticism causes resentment. There are much better psychological methods of teaching."

(4) "It is *ridiculous* to indulge my (bad habit) —because, if I cannot stop *one* bad habit, I will advertise my weakness to other bad habits seeking weak prey."

(5) "It would be *ridiculous* to think that the color of a person's skin limits that person's intellect, ability or personal capability to succeed."

(6) "It would be *ridiculous* to let an unhappy childhood experience affect my entire life."

(7) "It is *ridiculous* to try to carry the burdens of tomorrow's tasks, added to the burdens of today. I shall leave tomorrow's tasks for tomorrow. Sufficient unto each day are the burdens thereof."

(8) "It is *ridiculous* to waste even a minute thinking about someone I don't like. If I am not tolerant enough to forgive a person then, at least, I shall be sensible enough to ignore and forget him."

(9) "It is *ridiculous* to use the words: 'I demand' or 'we demand' because a demand creates instant resistance. It is much better to maintain a friendly attitude

of conciliation and negotiation, where everybody's point of view is respectfully considered, where everybody gives a little and gets a little, to achieve the hand-clasp of mutual resolution."

The preceding examples show how *ridicule* can be used in what psychologists call "affirmations" to associate in your mind any negative or undesirable traits with the idea that they are *ridiculous*.

Psychologically, you have very intense *revulsions* to anything which would make you *ridiculous*, or seem to be *ridiculous*, or even cause you to feel that you were acting or thinking in a *ridiculous* manner.

So, associating your negative and undesirable habits or traits with being *ridiculous* is an effective way to expel them from your life.

It is psychologically impossible to do anything which will make you *ridiculous*. So, if you want to stop doing something—label it "RIDICULOUS".

Chapter 78

Here's HELP! . . .

First, Reduce Or Remove
Any Opposition

The title of this chapter seems *obvious* enough.
That is precisely the problem!
It *obviously* should be desirable to first reduce
or remove any opposition which may block your progress
to your life-goal.

It is so *obvious* that most people neglect it!
They waste their efforts trying to remove *obstacles*—when
they need to remove the *opposition behind the obstacles!*

So let's begin at the beginning—which happens
to be a *Law of Physics:* "Any force, *however small,* will
move any mass, *however large,* if there is *no opposing
force.*"

Which is science's way of saying that it is smart
to reduce or remove the *opposition* behind the obstacles.
Then you can move obstacles by using only little effort!

It is easier to *reduce* or *remove* opposition than

it is to have to *exert constant effort against it every step of the way* to your goal.

It is even easier not to incur opposition in the first place!

If you trace your opposition back to its beginnings, you probably will find that *you caused it!* Something you did, said or wrote caused resentment. Once the seeds of resentment are planted, they grow into opposition . . .

UNLESS . . .

Unless you use *proven success methods* to turn resentment into goodwill. In its early stages, before resentment grows into opposition, resentment is easily turned into goodwill by the *proven success methods* in this and my other books.

Of course, even *after* resentment has grown into opposition, *proven success methods* can still *reduce* or *remove* the opposition.

This is much easier than having to *push against opposition* every step of the way to your life-goal.

For example:

Visualize that the path to your life-goal is entirely blocked by a large boulder. You are pushing the boulder from one side and your opposition is pushing back from the other side.

There is a limit to how hard you can push the boulder. So it is much easier to reduce or remove the opposing force—using *proven success methods*.

Then, it will be *easy* for you to push the boulder because it is a *Law of Physics* that:

"Any force, *however small*, will move any mass, *however large*, if there is *no opposing force*."

So, if you *remove the opposing force behind any obstacle* which is blocking your path to your goal, it will require very little effort on your part to push the *obstacle* aside—*because there will be no opposing force.*

By using the *proven success methods* in this and my other books, you not only will be able to *remove* opposition—*but you will persuade the opposition to come around to your side and help you push obstacles from your path to success!*

And, you can get the help of THE *Expert* in removing obstacles in people's lives.

The Bible teaches that *faith can move mountains. Infinity* is a real *obstacle-mover!*

Of course, it takes a lot of faith to move a mountain. And, quite frankly, I haven't moved any mountains, yet.

But, I *have* moved some formidable-looking obstacles which *seemed* like mountains when I was down, looking up at them.

And, I know a lot of people who have moved much bigger obstacles than I have.

It isn't difficult, really. You see, it is a well-proven *Law of Life* that "Whatever a man can *conceive* and *BELIEVE . . . man can achieve.*"

Chapter 79

Here's HELP! . . .

PERSONAL MAGNETISM FOR EVERYBODY! Easy Lessons—In The Following Chapters

YOU . . . no matter what your age, size, shape, personal appearance—can have PERSONAL MAGNET-ISM to positively attract *any* person or persons within your *"personal magnetic field"* (which you, yourself, establish).

There is a difference between *physical* attractiveness (which differs in everybody because of *each individual's different physical appearance*) and *magnetive* attractiveness, which is a *skill* that can be learned and used by *everybody—regardless of age or physical appearance*.

It is the purpose of this and the following series of chapters to teach the skill, the methods and techniques of PERSONAL MAGNETISM.

Remember, PERSONAL MAGNETISM is a *skill which can be learned*. Just as *any* skill can be learned.

There is nothing secret or mysterious about PERSONAL MAGNETISM. It is simply a matter of learning *what* to do and *how* to do it. Like learning anything else.

Anybody can learn it! Anybody can have a magnetic personality which positively will attract *any* other person or persons.

YOU can have a MAGNETIC PERSONALITY —*whatever your age! Age has absolutely nothing to do with personal magnetism!*

There are a lot of charming older women with happy faces wrinkled with smile-lines, who radiate exciting, attractive PERSONAL MAGNETISM which makes swim-suit models mere walking statues by comparison.

There are a lot of wonderful older men with a merry twinkle in their eyes as they look upon an inexperienced world with the tolerance of wisdom which comes only from having lived so much, so long. They radiate PERSONAL MAGNETISM which locker-room heroes will not be able to match for years.

There is no one age which is the "best" age for radiating a magnetic personality. Every age has its compensating advantages. If you learn the methods, techniques and lessons of the following series of chapters, you will happily discover that *every age is the best age to learn and use PERSONAL MAGNETISM!* And that the best time is NOW!

Nor does *physical appearance—outward* characteristics such as facial features, body size and shape— have any affect upon PERSONAL MAGNETISM, which is *generated inside* and is *intensified inside* before it can be *projected and radiated outside.*

Surely you must have seen actually thousands

of men and women in person and on television or in the movies who had *terrifically magnetic personalities* yet whose *physical characteristics* would not have earned them a back seat in a beauty or body contest.

Basically, in the simplest terms, PERSONAL MAGNETISM is deliberately *generated inside* and *intensified inside* as what personality counselors call an "INNER GLOW".

Then the "INNER GLOW" is deliberately *radiated and projected outside* as an "OUTER GLOW" which *irresistibly attracts others*—as selected individuals or as groups.

So no one should count himself or herself out because of age or personal appearance.

As the following series of chapters will teach: PERSONAL MAGNETISM IS FOR EVERYBODY!

Chapter 80

Here's HELP! . . .

PERSONAL MAGNETISM:
Eye Contact

Your *eyes* are so important in *radiating* and *projecting* your PERSONAL MAGNETISM that we shall devote the next several chapter-lessons to *"eye magnetism"*.

In this chapter: *Eye Contact!*

Your *eyes* are the *"windows of your mind"*.

Your *mind can look through your eyes* into the eyes—*and minds*—of others.

Others can use their eyes to *look through your eyes into your mind.*

In PERSONAL MAGNETISM, you must *look directly and deeply into the eyes of others.*

This is *"eye contact"* and, skillfully used, can be a *terrific magnetic force!*

As you will learn in later chapters, PERSONAL MAGNETISM is a composite of many factors—physical, mental, emotional—and each factor, skillfully used as taught, will be a part of your magnetic personality.

Probably, your *eyes* are the most important—because your *eyes* are your most effective way to *communicate* your PERSONAL MAGNETISM to a selected person or to a group.

Unless you *communicate* your personal magnetism to others, *you cannot attract them to you.*

The most effective way to *communicate* personal magnetism is through *eye contact.*

It is *eye contact* which is the *channel through which magnetic attraction flows*—from you to another and from another to you.

Without direct—*and deep*—eye contact, magnetic attraction is so difficult that it is greatly diminished, if not impossible.

Eye contact is established by looking directly and deeply into the eyes of another.

Important! Look *directly* and *deeply!* Do not stare! Do not glare! And do not aimlessly gaze!

Look *directly* and *deeply!*

Practice by looking into your own eyes in a mirror.

First impress on yourself, what NOT to do. *Stare* at your own eyes in the mirror. *Glare* at your own eyes in the mirror. The negative impression you will get will emphatically teach you NOT to *stare* or *glare* at another—*especially into his or her eyes.*

Then *gaze aimlessly* at your own eyes in the mirror. You will see reflected a memorable example of NOT projecting personal magnetism!

Now, by looking into your mirror, *look directly and deeply into your eyes.*

266

Looking *directly* is easy, although it is almost always neglected in real life *where indifference and aimlessness open NO magnetic channels!* But be careful not to *stare* as you *look directly*. Simply, forthrightly, *look directly*. Do not over-do it.

Looking *deeply* may require some practice. *Then, practice!* Practice looking *deeply* (without staring) into your own eyes in the mirror. Get the *"feel"* of looking *deeply*.

Practice looking away from your mirror and then looking back into it and instantly looking *directly* and *deeply* into your eyes.

Practice looking *more deeply* . . . and *more deeply* . . . and *more deeply!* (But do *not* use a *fixed intense stare*).

It is very important that you learn to look *directly* and *deeply* into the eyes of others—because this is *the all-important EYE CONTACT which communicates your PERSONAL MAGNETISM, your magnetic power to attract!*

Of course, you have to *have* PERSONAL MAGNETISM in order to *communicate* it. And that will be taught in following chapters. But this chapter on EYE CONTACT has been put first because it is what you need to know and *use* to project and radiate the increasing PERSONAL MAGNETISM you will acquire from the following chapters.

Through eye contact you can begin immediately to use each method as you learn it.

The preceding methods apply primarily to *eye contact with individuals* but they can in a more general manner be applied to *eye contact in speaking to groups.*

In projecting and radiating PERSONAL MAGNETISM in speaking to groups and even large audiences you *must* look *directly* and *deeply* into their *eyes.*

Do *not* speak to your audience as a *group of people.* Speak *directly* and *personally* to your audience as *individuals—and look directly and deeply into their eyes continuously throughout your speech.*

Do *not read* your speech. Do *not speak from notes* (except from a *brief outline*—hand-printed so large that you can refer to it at a glance, if you *absolutely must*).

It will help you, reassure you, convince you of the *absolute necessity of looking directly and deeply into the eyes of others,* if you will study the use of *eye contact* by watching the *eyes* (and *eye contact*) of the actors, actresses, highly-paid personalities, and leading commercial announcers on television. Do not pay attention to *what* they are saying—*concentrate intensely on their use of eye contact.*

You will learn quickly by watching actual demonstrations of *eye contact.* The television day-time serials, full-length movies, the top stars on television spectaculars, and the really good, big-name commercial announcers enable you to see continuous demonstrations of how the real pros in projecting PERSONAL MAGNETISM through *eye contact* do it by looking *directly* and *deeply* into the eyes of others.

Make a thorough study of these continuous television demonstrations of *eye contact*—and as you study the use of *eye contact* by each top performer, remember that he or she *is attracting millions of viewers! And attracting millions of dollars! That* is PERSONAL MAGNETISM!

Chapter 81

Here's HELP! . . .

PERSONAL MAGNETISM:
Eye Language

In the preceding chapter you learned the method of projecting PERSONAL MAGNETISM through EYE CONTACT—looking *directly* and *deeply* into the *eyes* of others.

You learned that *eye contact* was your "channel" of communicating *magnetically attractive thoughts* . . . from your eyes . . . *through* the eyes of others . . . *into their minds*—because "eyes are the *windows* of the mind".

In this chapter, you will learn to use EYE LANGUAGE by which you *directly communicate* your *magnetically attractive thoughts* from your eyes *through the eyes of others . . . into their minds.*

Psychologically, *thought transference* is called *"telepathy"*, however, I like to think of EYE LANGUAGE as being as much *physical* as mental—not so much *"telepathy"* as *actual physical communication,* using the eyes instead of the voice.

Actually, of course, EYE LANGUAGE is both physical and mental—and can be greatly intensified by emotion.

EYE LANGUAGE is most easily learned by practicing in front of your mirror so that you can *see* the actual *expression* in your eyes as *they convey your thought* to the "other person" which in mirror-practice is portrayed by your own reflection.

Practice EYE LANGUAGE as follows:

(1) Standing in front of your mirror, look *directly* and *deeply* into your eyes in the mirror, and intensely think: *"I like you!"* (Visualize that this thought is to be projected to *another person,* symbolized by your reflection in the mirror.)

(2) Now, while intensely thinking *"I like you!"*, express *"I like you!"* with your *eyes*—visualizing your reflection in the mirror as *another person* to whom you are projecting your EYE MESSAGE.

(3) Pretend that you cannot speak (or do not want to be overheard by others), and that you *must* express *"I like you!"* intensely, sincerely, convincingly— *ONLY with your eyes.*

(4) Continue practicing in EYE LANGUAGE *"I like you!"* to your reflection in the mirror (*which you visualize as another person* whom you want to understand your EYE MESSAGE: *"I like you!"*) until you *"feel"* that your EYE LANGUAGE is being *clearly* communicated.

(5) Make a list of *ten different personal messages* which you might use to *attract others* through the PERSONAL MAGNETISM of EYE LANGUAGE.

(6) Continue to practice these ten different

EYE MESSAGES in front of your mirror until you actually can *make your eyes "talk"*. Have no doubt that you can do it! All of the successful people who project and radiate PERSONAL MAGNETISM use EYE LANGUAGE frequently, every day, *often to reinforce the magnetic effect of their spoken words.*

(7) When, through practice in front of your mirror, you have learned to project EYE LANGUAGE—*start using it at every opportunity, every day.* Be sure to begin with EYE CONTACT—first, look *directly* and *deeply* into the person's eyes. Then, project your message through EYE LANGUAGE. Experiment at different distances to increase your *magnetic field* of attraction.

You will find that you now have a new and miraculous power—the *people-attracting power* of *eye-communication.*

And this is just *one* of the many rewarding methods of PERSONAL MAGNETISM!

More . . . in the next chapter . . .

Chapter 82

Here's HELP! . . .

PERSONAL MAGNETISM:
Smile With Your Eyes!

Most people *mistakenly* think that they should smile with their *mouths!*

Smiling with your mouth should be only the *last* part of a smile—and then only occasionally!

Really magnetic persons maintain a constant appearance of friendly good humor by smiling only occasionally with their mouths but *smiling always with their eyes!*

So this chapter-lesson will be devoted to one of the easiest, yet one of the most effective, techniques of PERSONAL MAGNETISM . . . *SMILE WITH YOUR EYES!*

If you try to *start* a smile with your lips and mouth, it will give you a phony, superficial look. Try it in front of your mirror—and see yourself as others see you! Then, *never again,* will you try to *start* a smile with your lips and mouth!

A genuine, sincere smile starts from *within* you—not from a fixed position of your lips.

You have to "feel" a smile before you can sincerely express it facially—and when you do start to express a smile, personality experts all insist that you *must start to smile with your eyes!*

That is a PERSONAL MAGNETISM rule: SMILE WITH YOUR EYES!

Try *that* in front of a mirror—and see a *new, magnetic YOU!*

First, maintain a constant attitude of *goodwill* and *good humor*—because *the constant expression of those two qualities* are the foundation upon which PERSONAL MAGNETISM is built.

Then, because of your constant attitude of goodwill and good humor, it is *natural* to "*feel*" like smiling to *express* your goodwill and good humor.

Begin your smile *naturally*—SMILE WITH YOUR EYES! Imagine a *humorous twinkle* in your eyes. Then intensify the twinkle until your *eyes are smiling!*

Smiling with one's *eyes* is not a new discovery of mine. It has been taught for years by all competent personality trainers, success counselors and dramatic schools. It even has been enshrined in song (remember the old song: "*When Irish EYES Are SMILING*"?).

There is a basic psychological reason for starting your smile, *first from the inside,* and *then with your eyes.* Psychologically, whenever you *consciously* try to express an *emotion* (unless you have had years of professional training as an actor or actress), *you become self-conscious.*

When you are self-conscious, as you will be,

you will look positively silly trying to "emote" even such a simple expression as a smile, if you begin (unnaturally) by curving your lips and, worse, by also baring your teeth!

So you must avoid that self-conscious, "curved-lips" expression—*by not thinking about your lips at all.*

You must not *think* about *any* facial expression. You just *"feel inside"* like smiling and you start expressing that pleasant feeling—*naturally*—beginning *with your eyes.*

Here's what happens (and you can check this in your mirror): As soon as you "inwardly feel" like smiling and start expressing that pleasant feeling with a good-humored twinkle in your *eyes,* your *entire* facial expression changes—in a genuinely *natural* manner—*without any conscious effort* on your part at all!

Your "smile lines" wrinkle automatically around your eyes. Your eyes, themselves, brighten—*and become more interesting and attractive.* Your lips relax and the corners of your mouth turn upward. Your cheeks lift, as does the entire expression of your face. In seconds— without any self-conscious forcing—you have a *natural,* pleasant, radiant, good-humored expression.

This good-humored, smiling-eyes expression usually is sufficient and generally preferable for most occasions.

However, if you feel like it, and the situation is appropriate, continue *naturally* into a big, broad, friendly smile. But, once you part your lips and show your teeth, *you've got to go all the way to a big, full smile.* Because, if you open your lips to smile and *only smile half-way,* you will have a self-conscious, simpering smirk.

274

The safest and best way is to maintain a constant attitude of goodwill and good-humor . . . so that your smile will begin *naturally* by your *inwardly feeling* like smiling . . . then start by *smiling with your eyes* . . . and let nature take it from there!

The importance of *how* a person smiles has been the subject of wise comment by the great thinkers for centuries.

Let me remind you of just two:

The famous author and editor of the 1800's, Christian Nestell Bovee, wrote: "Something of a person's *character* may be discovered by observing *how* he smiles. Some people never smile; they only grin."

A century earlier, the Swiss theologian, John Caspar Lavater, warned: *"A disagreeable smile is more repulsive than a frown."*

PERSONAL MAGNETISM requires an *attractive* smile, because that is what magnetism is—the power to *attract*.

Now, to your *magnetic, attractive smile*—let us add an amazing NEW discovery *which will enable you to magnetically use your voice with irresistible attraction!*

In the *next* chapter . . .

Chapter 83

Here's HELP! . . .

PERSONAL MAGNETISM: Project Your Voice Through Your Eyes!

This is *not* a lesson on the complex functions involved in speech. In this chapter, we shall *not* discuss tone initiation, pitch modulation, articulation, and the many proper operations of your vocal apparatus. That would require an entire book—and there already are many good books on the subject.

This chapter has only one purpose:
TO GIVE YOU A MAGNETIC VOICE!

To do this in the simplest, easiest way, we shall concentrate on only one voice function, *voice projection,* which simply is *how you deliver your spoken message* from you to others—individuals or groups.

Again to simplify, let us concede that the *sound* of your voice comes out of your mouth—at least, the *articulated words* do. That is *physical.*

However, the *control* of your voice *projection* is *mental.*

You actually *think* how and where you want to *project* your voice. And by your *thinking,* you control all of the subconscious functions which are much too rapid and complex to be handled by your conscious mind.

To expand an example from a preceding chapter, when you *think* and *feel* that you are *projecting* and *directing* your *spoken message* into the EYES of a person, you are greatly intensifying *eye-contact,* which is taught in that chapter.

As you learned, the way to establish and maintain *eye-contact,* is to look *directly* and *deeply* into the EYES of a person. This greatly increases your own PERSONAL MAGNETISM, *your magnetic power to attract and influence others.*

To use your VOICE magnetically—you project your VOICE directly and deeply into the EYES of others—from your own EYES!

Here's how to do it:

You do *not think or feel* that your voice is being projected from your *mouth*—but, instead, *you intensely think and feel that your voice is being magnetically projected through your EYES directly and deeply into the EYES of others.*

You can *think* your voice projection is *from wherever* you wish and you will *feel* your voice projection *is wherever you think it is.*

For example, various speech trainers teach many different voice projection-placements according to the speakers' needs (and the speech teachers own personal theories).

A frequent speech problem is that the speaker "speaks from his throat" by over-use of his throat muscles in projecting (or, in this case, *not* projecting) his voice. There are physical exercises in speech therapy to overcome this speech problem which is called "throatiness". But since the purpose of this chapter is not physical speech therapy, we shall limit it to simple psychological techniques.

The psychology of "getting your voice out of your throat" simply is to *think* and *feel* that you are *projecting your voice from someplace other than your throat.*

Here are several examples of *psychological* voice projection techniques to eliminate "throatiness" and "mouthing".

(1) *Think* and *feel* that you are projecting your voice from your *forehead*. This gets your voice "*out of your throat,*" gives it "lift," and greatly improves tone and resonance, especially if you practice "*humming*" tone-placement.

(2) The wife of a former President decided to "go public" and, because this required frequent speaking, she took speech lessons. She was taught to "*speak six inches in front of her mouth*". This got her voice *out of her throat, mouth and nose.*

(3) A helpful technique in public speaking to large audiences is to *begin* your speech by *thinking, feeling and directing your voice to the person farthest from you.* This was a requirement in the days before public address systems amplified your voice to an equal level for all listeners. It still is a good technique because even though you no longer need projection *volume*, it gives you a *feeling* of "*range*" and "*out-reach*".

The foregoing examples are given, not to teach

speech, although they are useful—but to emphasize the basic principles to be used by this chapter *to give you a MAGNETIC VOICE:*

(1) You can *project* your voice *from* any part of your face—throat, mouth, lips, the back of your upper front teeth (which is good tone placement), your forehead (much better tone placement) *and you can project your voice through and from your EYES* (which is the first half of this chapter's lesson). You do this simply by *thinking HOW your voice is being projected—and feeling that it IS being projected exactly as your thoughts direct.*

(2) Not only can you project your voice *from* your EYES—but you also can control *where* (the exact place) *you want your voice to be received.*

Thus, you can project your voice *through and from your EYES directly and deeply into the EYES of others—simply by thinking and feeling that you are doing so!* The effect is hypnotically magnetic!

You will remember that preceding chapter-lessons taught that *looking* directly and deeply into the EYES of others (*eye-contact*) greatly intensified your PERSONAL MAGNETISM and enabled you to use magnetic *eye language.*

Now, by EYE to EYE *voice* communication, you can further intensify and project your PERSONAL MAGNETISM.

It is so important that you learn to project your voice *through* and *from* your EYES and impress your words directly and deeply *into* the EYES of others, and *through* their EYES *into* their MINDS—that we shall briefly review exactly how to do it.

You can choose and control the manner of projecting your voice.

You project your voice *through* and *from* your EYES—simply by *thinking* that your voice *is being* projected *through* and *from* your EYES, and by *feeling* your voice *actually being* projected *through* and *from* your EYES.

Your *thinking* and *feeling* completely *control the source* of your voice projection. So, *think* and *feel* your voice projection *through* and *from* your EYES.

Similarly, you can choose and control *where* (the exact place) you want your voice to be *projected* and *received most intensely.*

You project your voice *directly* and *deeply into* the EYES of others—simply by *thinking* and *feeling* that your voice *is being* projected *directly* and *deeply into* the EYES of others.

Because *"eyes are the windows of the mind"*, you actualy project your voice *through* their EYES *into* their MINDS.

This, of course, is the basis of *hypnotism.*

But this series of chapter-lessons concerns PERSONAL MAGNETISM—*which is sufficiently powerful, itself,* as you learn how to generate an INNER GLOW!

In the next chapter . . .

Chapter 84

Here's HELP! . . .

PERSONAL MAGNETISM:
Generate An INNER GLOW . . .
Radiate An OUTER GLOW!

You cannot radiate personal magnetism *you do not have!*

So the first step is to *generate* personal magnetism so that you *have* it to radiate.

This means that you must generate *inside you* what magnetic personalities think of as an "INNER GLOW."

An INNER GLOW is a combination of physical, mental and emotional "feelings" which, together, generate personal magnetism . . . your INNER GLOW.

To avoid the complexities of technical explanations, we shall limit this only to the few simple things you *need* to know—specifically, HOW to do it:

(1) Generating the INNER GLOW of per-

sonal magnetism is done by consciously, deliberately *arousing within you a "feeling"* which combines alertness, excitement, exhilaration, elation, anticipation, confidence and emotional radiance.

(2) You must be *intensely aware* of a surging *build-up within you* of this combination of "feelings."

(3) This *intensification* of "feelings" must create *inner pressure for release.*

(4) Personal magnetism is generated by *"feeling" this intense inner pressure—but deliberately restraining it.*

(5) This will generate a vibrant *inner tenseness* which is the INNER GLOW of *intense* alertness, excitement, exhilaration, elation, anticipation, confidence and emotional radiance—*restrained* and *controlled,* but ready for *magnetic projection* by you to attract an individual or group.

(6) It is this *restraint* of *intense emotional pressure* which generates personal magnetism as an INNER GLOW that can be radiated and projected as an OUTER GLOW to *attract* others.

(7) Personal magnetism is not generated by just reading about it. *It has to be developed by actual practice.* Here's HOW:

(a) Practice arousing *intense feelings* of alertness, excitement, exhilaration, elation, anticipation, confidence and emotional radiance.

(b) Begin by practicing arousing these feelings—*intensely, one at a time,* while you are alone, preferably in a quiet place where there are no distractions.

(c) Make a written list of these feelings. Write

them on a small card or piece of paper which you can carry with you to review in spare moments.

(d) List the feelings you want to practice arousing—in the following order: alertness, excitement, exhilaration, elation, anticipation, confidence and emotional radiance.

(e) Then, practice . . . practice . . . practice *arousing* and *intensifying* each feeling—one at a time:

(f) Feel ALERT! Feel a keen sense of *awareness* of yourself and your surroundings. *Feel watchful . . . ready . . . ready to act . . . ready to respond . . . instantly!*

(g) Feel a keen sense of EXCITEMENT! Come alive! *Feel a thrill running through your nervous system!* Breathe faster!

(h) Feel EXHILARATED! Feel *enlivened!* Feel *stimulated!* Give yourself an *emotional lift! Step up your emotional charge!*

(i) Feel ELATED! *Feel flushed with success!* Feel *exhalted, in high spirits!*

(j) Feel ANTICIPATION! Feel that *"something wonderful"* is about to happen—and that *your personal magnetism is going to make it happen!*

(k) Feel CONFIDENT! *Very* confident! Feel that you are going to get what you want! Feel that you are going to do what you want to do! *Nobody and nothing can stop you!* You are *sure* of yourself! *Absolutely sure!*

(l) Feel EMOTIONAL RADIANCE! Feel that you are *magnetically radiating attraction power— emotionally!* Feel that you are a powerful *emotional magnet . . . attracting! . . . attracting! . . . attracting!* Know that others feel the radiance of your emotional power . . . that your personal magnetism surrounds you like an aura . . . that anyone—*everyone*—near you will *intensely feel* your magnetism . . . *attracting!* . . . *attracting!* . . . *attracting!*

(m) Practice *arousing within you* the feelings which *combine* to generate personal magnetism—as just described: *alertness . . . excitement . . . exhilaration . . . elation . . . anticipation . . . confidence . . . emotional radiance.*

Practice *arousing within you* each feeling, separately—one at a time—in the order stated.

Then, when you can *arouse* within you each feeling at will—at your mental command—practice *intensifying* each feeling until you generate *pressure for release.*

Now, *combine* all of the *intensified* feelings and you will have achieved the INNER GLOW of personal magnetism!

The next step is the *controlled release* of your INNER GLOW of personal magnetism as a *radiant* and *directly projected* OUTER GLOW.

Since you have generated the *intense pressure* of an INNER GLOW of personal magnetism *within you* —you can *release* it . . . *radiate* it . . . *project* it . . . by *mental command,* simply by *feeling* that you are doing so.

Thus, you *radiate* and *project* the OUTER GLOW of your magnetic personality.

Remember that *personal magnetism is generated by intense emotional pressure under restraint.* It is radiated and projected by *your focusing it* on the individual or group which you want to *attract* and then by your *releasing* your personal magnetism in *whatever degree of intensity* you desire.

Personal magnetism is the power to *attract*—so always *intensely feel* that you are *attracting* . . . *attracting* . . . *attracting!*

Personal magnetism has an *"electric"* quality. Indeed, magnetic science is based primarily on electricity. And, electrical science is based substantially on magnetic attraction.

Electrodynamics is the branch of physics which deals with the forces of *"electrical attraction."*

Electromagnetism is a branch of science which is devoted entirely to the *relationship of electricity and magnetism.*

Life, itself, is thought to be a composite of electromagnetic forces!

So, certainly you should think of your *personal magnetism* as having an *"electric"* quality.

You will increase your "feeling" of *personal magnetism* by thinking of it in *"electric"* terms . . . radiation . . . magnetic wave projection . . . dynamic attraction . . . surrounding yourself with an *electromagnetic field* . . . and *your* being a *generator of electromagnetism* which attracts others when you "turn on the power".

When you mentally and emotionally put *electricity* into your *personal magnetism* you radiate a new and vibrant power!

Then . . . increase your magnetic voltage!

In the next chapter, you will learn an entirely different method of *attracting others.* You will learn to *attract others* by *fulfilling their subconscious needs.*

There is *magnetic power UNLIMITED* . . . in the next chapter . . .

Chapter 85

Here's HELP! . . .

PERSONAL MAGNETISM: Attract Others By Fulfilling Their Subconscious Needs

Here is a *different* kind of personal magnetism —*and it is personal magnetism UNLIMITED!*

In preceding chapters, you learned to generate an INNER GLOW (a combination of intensified "feelings" within you—pressing for release) and then to radiate and project your INNER GLOW to others as an OUTER GLOW of personal magnetism which would *attract* individuals or groups—physically, mentally, emotionally.

Now, you will learn the PERSONAL MAGNETISM of being a *"source of fulfillment"*.

By fulfilling the deep (subconscious) *needs* of others, you *attract* them to you as a *"source of fulfillment"*.

Just as hungry people *seek a source* of food to *fulfill their need* and satisfy their hunger, so people who are "hungry" for appreciation, or a feeling of importance, or the feeling of being needed, or other deep, subconscious *needs—seek a source who will fulfill those needs.*

By establishing *yourself* as a *source of fulfillment* of the deep, subconscious *needs* of others—you become *irresistibly attractive* to them!

This is because, whether they realize "why" or not, THEY NEED YOU!

Let us use a typical example:

All people (even those who deny it) have a compelling subconscious *need to feel important.* So, if every time *you* see, phone or write them, you say, write or do something *which makes them feel important*—they are irresistibly *attracted to you* as a dependable *source of fulfilling their need to feel important.*

The PERSONAL MAGNETISM of being a *source of fulfillment* is just as simple as that!

In fact, it is so simple that few people realize the *irresistible attraction* of being a *source of fulfillment,* and therefore neglect this opportunity for PERSONAL MAGNETISM, *UNLIMITED!*

Few people realize how deeply compelling are certain subconscious needs of others. Most people do not even know what these certain compelling subconscious needs are!

So . . . the following information will give *you* a great advantage over most other people.

You will know the compelling subconscious needs of others. And, by knowing, you can establish *yourself* as a dependable *source of fulfillment* of these compelling needs.

287

This will make you *irresistibly attractive* to others—as the *source of fulfilling their compelling subconscious needs.*

There is no greater magnetic power!

Here's HELP! . . .

Here is a list of some of the most compelling subconscious needs of others. We have selected those which you—or anyone—can most easily fulfill and thereby become a *source of fulfillment* which will make you *irresistibly attractive* to them.

(1) The need to feel ACCEPTED

This need, *when unfulfilled,* has been and still is one of the principal causes of racial hostility, and of resentment by most minority groups—although being *denied acceptance* is by no means limited to minority groups.

When *acceptance is denied,* the *rejected* person, group, race or nationality feels *discriminated against* and responds with resentment, anger, hostility and, sometimes, violence. This, of course, makes them *even less acceptable.*

The way to be accepted—*is to be acceptable.* Being acceptable cannot be gained by threats or legislation. *Being acceptable must be deserved.*

So . . . how do *you* become a *source of fulfillment* of the need of others to feel ACCEPTED? Two ways:

(a) Help them *deserve* acceptance

(b) Then, give them the reality of genuine acceptance by *openly accepting them yourself,* and by helping them win the acceptance of others.

Most people have an inferiority complex to

some extent. One of the prinicpal symptoms is the feeling (often false) of not really being *accepted*.

When you fulfill—or help fulfill—their need to feel *accepted*, you establish yourself as a *source of fulfillment*, the benefits of which are almost unlimited!

(2) The need for APPROVAL

Everyone (except the arrogant egocentric) needs *approval*. So fill that need by sincerely and, when appropriate, enthusiastically, expressing *approval* . . . as often as possible . . . in as many different ways as possible . . . to as many people as possible.

Do not wait to be asked. *Volunteer your approval* of people's work, accomplishments, appearance, families, homes, whatever you possibly can find to *approve*.

Express sincere, enthusiastic *approval* often and to everybody and—*presto!*—you will have the magic of *personal magnetism, unlimited!*

(3) The need to feel ADMIRED

There is something in everyone—and much in many people—which you can find to sincerely *admire*.

Find it . . . and sincerely express your *admiration*. Do not limit your expressions of *admiration* to the individuals, themselves. Include their families, homes, furniture, clothing, everything and anything you can find to *admire*.

In fact, *make a career out of expressing admiration!* If you do it sincerely, you cannot over-do it. *People need the lift of sincere admiration!*

(4) The need to be APPRECIATED

Appreciation means two different things.

One is the *expression of gratitude*.

The other is the *awareness of worth*.

Do not neglect either in fulfilling the need to be *appreciated*. People bestow their favors upon those who always show the most gratitude. People seek the companionship of those who hold them in the highest esteem.

Make yourself a *source* of *abundant gratitude* and *visible esteem*. Your *personal magnetism* will increase to the extent that you do this.

(5) The need to feel IMPORTANT

This was used as an example earlier in this chapter, but the need to feel IMPORTANT is so compelling that it is included in this list to be sure it is not overlooked.

You can develop a terrifically *magnetic personality* just by establishing yourself as a *source for fulfilling* a feeling of IMPORTANCE in *every person you meet . . . at every opportunity . . . always . . . without exception!*

You will, indeed, have acquired *personal magnetism, unlimited!*

(6) The need to receive ATTENTION

People will do almost *anything* to get *attention*. The daily news is filled with examples: demonstrations, protest marches, prison riots, ridiculous clothing (or no clothing!), all sorts of weird activities, with the tragic ultimate being the soaking of clothes with gasoline and setting themselves on fire in a flaming sacrifice on the altar of ATTENTION!

The compelling subconscious need for ATTENTION is so uncompromising that you short-circuit your magnetic attraction the instant you do not give others the *attention* they need, want, or think they deserve.

And, of course, the opposite is true. You *increase your magnetic attraction* in direct proportion to your willingness and ability to give your *sincere, interested attention to people,* and *their* conversation, *their* ideas, *their* accomplishments, and the many things which are important to *them.*

There are many more subconscious needs which you must fulfill in others, if you are to fully develop the amazing potential of this kind of *personal magnetism, UNLIMITED.* An entire *section* of my book, *How To Get Whatever You Want,* is devoted exclusively to this important subject, with a *separate chapter on each of the foregoing needs* which are only briefly described here—and other needs which, if you fulfill them in others, *you will unlock their minds and their hearts!*

But there is a miraculous POWER which is far greater than personal magnetism—because *without this POWER you will surely fail*—and *with this POWER you will abundantly succeed!*

In the next chapter, you will learn this motivating POWER *which assures success in personal relationships . . . in business . . . and in all areas of life!*

In the next chapter . . .

Chapter 86

Here's HELP! ...

The Power Of CARING ENOUGH!

William James, the Harvard philosopher and psychologist, and perhaps the greatest thinker of modern times, wrote:

"If you only CARE ENOUGH for the result, you will almost certainly attain it. If you wish to be rich, you will be rich; if you wish to be learned, you will be learned; if you wish to be good, you will be good. *Only you must REALLY wish these things."*

Yes, as William James stated: *"If you only CARE ENOUGH for the result, you will almost certainly attain it."*

That is how to become whatever you want to be in life. *You must CARE ENOUGH!*

That is how to achieve your life-goal. *You must CARE ENOUGH!*

That is the power *to become . . . to get . . . to achieve!* It is the power of CARING ENOUGH!

The power to succeed . . . to attain . . . to

achieve . . . is *fueled by desire* . . . white-hot desire which burns itself into your subconscious . . . which sears its brand on your every thought and action . . . which is your overwhelming obsession!

You must CARE ENOUGH!

In my book, *Thoughts To Build On*, there is an old fable concering a dog that bragged about his speed as a runner. One day the dog chased a rabbit but failed to catch it.

The other dogs made fun of him but he explained, "Remember, the rabbit was running for his life, while I was running only for the fun of chasing him."

In that fable, you will find one of the most valuable lessons for success in life. It is the power of your CARING ENOUGH.

In the fable just told, the dog did not catch the rabbit because the dog did not really CARE ENOUGH. How many opportunities have *you* missed or wasted because *you* did not CARE ENOUGH?

In the fable, the rabbit, *did* CARE ENOUGH. It was a matter of life or death! The rabbit *tried harder!*

You must CARE ENOUGH to *try harder!*

There is *success-magic* in those two words: TRY HARDER!

I witnessed an interview with billionaire J. Paul Getty during which he was asked the secret of success. Here is his *billion-dollar secret* in two words: "TRY HARDER!"

If you *really* CARE ENOUGH, you will *try harder* . . . and then *try harder* than that . . . and then *try much harder* . . . *constantly* . . . so that you pyramid your efforts and thus pyramid your gains.

"Surely," you say, "Success must be more complex than *that!*"

No. Really, it isn't.

And I tell you this from a lifetime of practical business experience. I have been president of eight corporations and success counsel to 102 companies.

So I have had a lifetime of *inside, top-level* business experience. I have been *"in"* on decades of *top* business decisions.

And I have had *inside* knowledge of the business *efforts* of thousands of *suppliers*, large and small, who supplied or serviced the many corporations with which I have been directly or indirectly associated.

So, the following conclusions are based on inside, top-level knowledge, experience and first-hand observation over many years.

(1) Very, very few corporations *really* CARE ENOUGH . . . so they do *not try harder.*

(2) Very, very few executives *really* CARE ENOUGH . . . so they do *not try harder.*

(3) Even fewer other employees *really* CARE ENOUGH . . . so they do *not try harder.*

(4) *Routine effort* by most corporations, by most executives, and by almost all other employees is *standard, usual procedure.* They survive and often prosper *only* because their competition does not CARE ENOUGH and does not *try harder,* either.

So . . .

If *you* really CARE ENOUGH to *try harder* . . . and then *try harder* than that . . . and *then try much harder* . . . *constantly* . . . YOU will be so unusual, so exceptional, and so outstanding that your instant success will be assured and *you will be so greatly in demand that you can fill in the amount of your own pay check!*

Here is OPPORTUNITY UNLIMITED right at your finger tips—*now!*

All you have to do is *do what other people are too indifferent to do:*

CARE ENOUGH . . . *to try harder* . . . and *try harder* than that . . . and then *try much harder* . . . *continuously pyramiding your efforts . . . so that you constantly pyramid your gains!*

Will you? . . . Do you? . . . CARE ENOUGH?

Chapter 87

Here's HELP! ...

The Extra Power Of A WORTHY COMPELLING REASON

Here is *extra power* to enable you to get whatever you want—*faster!*

It is called the *Extra Power of a WORTHY COMPELLING REASON.*

Of course, you will get whatever you want by using intense mental pictures, reinforced by frequent mental goal-commands, and by using the other PROVEN SUCCESS METHODS taught in this and my other books —and you will get what you want *whether you have a WORTHY COMPELLING REASON or not.*

You will succeed by using the *only sure way to succeed:* OBTAIN AND USE AS MANY PROVEN SUCCESS METHODS AS POSSIBLE. That is the *only* requirement for succeeding.

Anybody can succeed simply by doing that.

Frankly, I am sorry that this is so.

I wish that this *sure way to succeed* would work *only* for good, deserving people with noble and worthy goals.

But it will work for *anyone* who *uses* it.

For example:

Suppose you want to be a millionaire just in order to be lazy, own a large estate, have all the expensive luxuries wealth can buy, and just loaf while servants bring you highballs.

You will get your million dollars by using the PROVEN SUCCESS METHODS taught in this and my other books—not because your *goal* is worthy, but because your *methods* assure certain success.

But, if you use the million dollars *solely for selfish purposes,* it will not bring you happiness but, instead, will bring you much trouble.

Your troubles would result, not from your *having* a million dollars, but because you *used it solely for selfish purposes.* The large amount of money simply would increase the opportunities for trouble. The *cause* would be selfishness which always brings trouble, *whatever* amount of money is used selfishly.

Now, to continue our example of your wanting to be a millionaire:

Whatever your reason for wanting a million dollars, you can get your million by constantly and intensely projecting *"millionaire" mental pictures into your subconscious,* reinforcing your *"millionaire" mental pictures* with mental *"Make a million!"* goal-commands, and using the other PROVEN SUCCESS METHODS in my books.

Your subconscious is not a moral judge; it is a cybernetic power which will materialize your mental pictures into reality.

Your subconscious does not judge whether what it produces is good or bad for you. Its function is not to judge, but to produce. It will materialize in your life *whatever* you mentally picture—which could be failure, poverty, sickness, immoral or criminal activities—*whatever you mentally picture!*

That is why this book has warned against "thinking poor" or "thinking failure," and has emphasized that you will become or get *whatever* you mentally picture —*good or bad.*

That is why this book continues to emphasize that for thousands of years all religions and philosophies— and now, more recently, modern science and psychology— have taught that *everyone's life is the product of his or her predominant thoughts (mental pictures)—for better or worse.*

With that background, let us now consider the *Extra Power of a WORTHY COMPELLING REASON.*

And let us do so, continuing to use our example of your wanting to be a millionaire.

If you want to be a millionaire *merely to loaf in idle luxury,* your subconscious will still respond to your mental pictures and mental goal-commands and other PROVEN SUCCESS METHODS—and will guide you to or attract to you the million dollars—*IF you can generate and maintain the necessary INTENSE DESIRE.*

BUT . . .

You will *lack* the inspiration, the motivation

and the *extra power of a WORTHY COMPELLING REASON*.

And *without* that inspiration, motivation and *extra power* of a *WORTHY COMPELLING REASON*:

(1) You will *lose* the *Power of CARING ENOUGH*.

(2) Your success drive *will not be fueled* by a white-hot desire which burns your mental pictures deeply into your subconscious and gives compelling authority to your mental goal-commands.

(3) You *will not feel the urgency* to obtain and use as many PROVEN SUCCESS METHODS as possible.

SO . . .

Even though your subconscious has the capability, you may not be able to generate and maintain the necessary INTENSE DESIRE POWER to command it— if you do not have a *WORTHY COMPELLING REASON* for what you want.

HOWEVER . . .

If, for example, you want a million dollars to use in establishing a Foundation to supply needed money to help others, if you want to help the underprivileged, or establish scholarships for ambitious students, or make grants in the fields of medical research, or use a substantial part of your wealth to help any of thousands of *worthy* causes—then you thereby give your success drive the *extra power of a WORTHY COMPELLING REASON*.

This applies, of course, not just to the worthy uses of acquired wealth, but to *all worthy goals,* whatever their nature.

For example:

If your goal is to attain *leadership*, not just for "boss-power", but to organize and lead a *worthy cause*—your success drive will have the *extra power of a WORTHY COMPELLING REASON*.

If your goal is to become *influential*, not just for "power-over-people", but to influence others to join in a *worthy cause*—you will have the motivation and persuasion of the *extra power of a WORTHY COMPELLING REASON*.

If your goal is to acquire advanced education, not just to *obtain* knowledge, but to *impart* knowledge to others through teaching and/or writing, or to *use* your advanced knowledge for the benefit of mankind, you will have the perserverance and dedication of the *extra power of a WORTHY COMPELLING REASON*.

Additional examples are not necessary. It is obvious that you greatly increase your power to achieve your life-goal—*if your goal is worthy*.

To refer to the preceding chapter, you will have a *worthy* goal about which you will CARE ENOUGH—which the great William James said would enable you to attain *any* goal. His statement is representative of all conclusive wisdom throughout civilization: *You can achieve your goal if you really CARE ENOUGH*.

Now, when you add to the *power of CARING ENOUGH*, the *extra power of a WORTHY COMPELLING REASON*, you generate a terrific success drive of enormous power!

And . . . there is even more!

You will add an unusual power with miraculous consequences . . . in the next chapter . . .

300

Chapter 88

Here's HELP! . . .

The Amazing Power Of OVER-BELIEF!

As psychologist William James taught at Harvard, everyone can and *should* hold what psychologist James called "OVER-BELIEFS" in one's ultimate achievements and goal attainments.

This is a profound psychological method which is of great importance to your present and your future. I urge you to study it thoroughly.

Reaffirming the manifest conclusion of religion and philosophy throughout the centuries, and its modern confirmation by science and psychology, it was William James who stated it categorically and concisely:

"BELIEF CREATES THE ACTUAL FACT."

Affirming, as it does, the conclusion arrived at by the great thinkers over a period of several thousand years, that clear, concise statement should be the cornerstone in building the future of each of us.

"BELIEF CREATES THE ACTUAL FACT."

But the brilliant mind of psychologist William James added something more—for which mankind can be forever grateful. He added the psychological power of OVER-BELIEF.

The need for OVER-BELIEF is obvious. Most people just cannot *believe* that they are capable of beginning from what may be a lowly present condition and rising to great heights of accomplishment.

Many people think that, because they are poor, they are condemned to poverty. They cannot—or do not—*believe* that they can become rich as the result of their own thinking and effort. They *think poor,* so they *remain poor.*

Their children are born and reared in poverty. *It is their life-style and so it becomes their life.* And becomes the lives of their children . . . and their children's children.

Thus the age-old poverty cycle continues until it is *broken by belief* that, for example, by using PROVEN SUCCESS METHODS, they can rise from poverty and become rich or famous or whatever they want to become.

This same kind of illustration can be used concerning the under-educated who just cannot *believe* that they can attain the most advanced education and become leaders and benefactors of mankind.

And this same kind of illustration can be used to describe all of the various kinds and conditions of people who just cannot *believe* that they can greatly improve their situation, much less attain wealth, fame, power and achieve some really outstanding goal in life.

You will note that, in every instance, the lack of advancement is due, *first, to lack of belief.*

302

It is the great tragedy of our time—as it has been for all the generations preceding us—that most people just do not *believe* they can do what, in fact, *they can do with absolute certainty and relative ease*—get *whatever* they want in life.

Even in those people who begin to develop some belief in themselves, their belief is too weak and uncertain to achieve greatly encouraging results. So the quick-quitters quit. And the others attain only mediocre results.

What is the cure for weak, uncertain belief?

OVER-BELIEF!

And what is this magic OVER-BELIEF?

OVER-BELIEF is *intensely believing* that you will accomplish *much more* than your *present* conditions *seem* to justify.

How do you OVER-BELIEVE?

Here's Help! . . .

(1) You cannot judge your future by your present.

(2) Since you cannot judge your future by your present, there is absolutely no reason why you should not OVER-BELIEVE that you will accomplish *much more* than you now UNDER-BELIEVE you can.

(3) Therefore, you should OVER-BELIEVE that you will be *much more* successful in achieving your life-goal—so that your life-goal becomes *bigger, better, more worthy.*

(4) The technique of OVER-BELIEF is to really "let yourself go" . . . go "all-out" . . . do not just OVER-BELIEVE *a little,* but OVER-BELIEVE *big* . . . OVER-BELIEVE *to the farthest limit of your imagination!*

(5) You will be amazed to see your OVER-

BELIEF change from an "impossible dream" to a *realizable future!*

It is our reliable *Law of Consistency* in action, again.

The Law of Consistency assures that what you actually accomplish MUST be and WILL be CONSISTENT (the same as) what you believe or OVER-BELIEVE you will accomplish.

It is a *Law of Life*.
It cannot be otherwise.
You can depend on it.

Chapter 89

Here's HELP! . . .

The Secret Of Goal-Achieving

The way to reach your goal in life is very simple. You can achieve *any* goal you choose!

Achieving your goal . . . *any* goal . . . *whatever* goal you choose . . . requires that you do several very simple things which *anybody* can easily do.

(1) *Fall forward!*

Everyone stumbles on the way to a goal. Sometimes you will fall. You will fall over *little* things. Nobody gets tripped up by a mountain, but only by something so small it was not noticed. (There's a lesson there!)

So when you do fall occasionally—always fall *forward . . . toward your goal!*

That, of course, is not a physical thing. It is a mental attitude. It is the attitude of *"persisting in progressing"* toward your goal even when you fall.

This leads to another form of persistence in goal-achieving:

(2) *Get up—when you fall down!*

Again, this is not physical, but mental. It is the mental attitude of taking the falls along the way to your life-goal as "mere happenings"—*not disasters!*

Don't just lie there and think that the road to your goal must be too rough because you fall so often.

Don't just lie there and think that "somebody tripped you".

Don't just lie there—GET UP!

Get up—when you fall down!

Get up—and GET GOING! *Toward your goal!*

The next step in goal-achieving is found in an old Japanese proverb:

(3) *"When you fall down, do not get up empty-handed!"*

When you gain something every time you fall —you learn to *"win even when you lose".*

When you learn how to *"win even when you lose",* you have learned the PROVEN SUCCESS METHOD of *failing your way to success.*

This method is so important and so effective that I wrote an entire chapter: "How To FAIL Your Way To SUCCESS" in my book *How To Get Whatever You Want.*

And, in the book you now are reading, the method is referred to in several chapters. So I shall not repeat the details here except to emphasize that failure is an accepted procedure in experimenting, research, testing and all scientific forms of "finding out".

Briefly here, because it is described in other chapters, the scientific method of *failing your way to suc-*

cess is keep finding out what won't work (and eliminate *that*) until you find out what will work (and do *that*). It is the method used in all scientific and industrial research.

So, instead of thinking of failure as something to be feared and avoided, you should realize that *failure is one of the most widely used research techniques*—and is a sure way to success.

If you succeed all of the time, it does not prove that you have ability. It merely proves that you have set your life-goal too low to be meaningful—*because you are afraid of failing*.

Timid people, who are afraid of failing, *lower their goals to their own low level of performance*.

They are like the novice golfer who cannot make par, and instead of improving his performance, *tries to change par* to conform to his own incompetence.

When you try to "win" in life by setting your life-goal so low that your constant improvement is not required—you do not really "win" because your life-prize is mediocrity. "Achieving" mediocrity is not "winning" anything. *It is not achievement; it is surrender.*

Anybody can attain mediocrity—and *most people do*. Why?

Because most people begin with low goals in life—or no goals at all. Or they quickly lower their goals at their first failure.

It isn't because they are lazy. Most mediocre people *work hard* at their mediocre jobs, for mediocre pay, to support their mediocre life-style—to conform to their low goal or no goal in life.

No, it isn't because they are lazy.

Nor is it because they are *under*-privileged or *under*-educated or any or all of the "*under*" designations usually used to describe so-called "deprived" persons.

Except one "*under*" characteristic:

They are under-motivated!

Because they are *under-motivated*, they set low goals or no goals for their lives.

Having low goals or no goals, they have nothing for which to use PROVEN SUCCESS METHODS and therefore can not and do not achieve any noteworthy success in life. They settle for mediocrity or less.

The obvious reason—the reason which everybody sees—is that people settle for mediocrity or less because they are *under-motivated*.

And, of course, that is *one* principal reason.

But the real, underlying deterrent of people who do not strive for *big success*—for big, challenging, worthy goals in life—*is that they are afraid they will fail!*

If people only would learn that failure is not something to fear, but something to *use as a means of succeeding!*

As described in the preceding part of this chapter, *failure is simply the means of finding out what will not work so that it can be eliminated in the search for what will work.* Failure is the principal research method used in all scientific, medical and industrial research.

Why should *you* be afraid of failure when *business spends billions of dollars* on research which business *knows in advance will fail most of the time?*

Edison and his staff conducted 17,000 experiments which *failed* before they *succeeded in the one ex-*

periment which enabled them to extract latex in substantial quantities from just *one* variety of plant! Which was *worth* the 17,000 failures!

In addition to being a PROVEN SUCCESS METHOD, failure is good for your character and personality. It is a *challenging* experience.

Failure does not take something *out* of you; *failure builds a lot of necessary character and personality qualities into you.* You are not weaker because you fail; you are tougher, stronger, more determined—and *much wiser!*

Somehow, I learned the foregoing fact when I was a very young man. So I set out to learn to "take" the hardest knocks of failure—*by deliberately exposing myself to failure situations.*

In athletics, I competed against superior opponents. As a young, amateur boxer, I worked out with the pros. I practiced house-to-house, "cold-canvass" selling until I got so accustomed to hearing the word "NO!" that it became an impersonal part of the *Law of Averages.*

So I am not writing about failure from an ivory tower. I have had a lot of experience with failure.

From my own lifetime of many failures and many successes, the lesson comes loud and clear:

My successes improved my situation—*but only my failures improved ME!* Failure is a great teacher.

Being unafraid of failure, you can seek the highest goal! *You may not reach the stars, but you can chart your course by them!*

Chapter 90

Here's HELP! . . .

What Is Your Most Valuable Personal Quality?

Suppose someone asked you, "What is your most valuable *personal quality?*"

What *personal quality* do you *now have* which is most valuable to you?

What is the most valuable *personal quality* which you *can acquire?*

Thomas Huxley, the great English scientist, stated, "The most valuable trait that you can acquire is the ability to *make yourself do the thing you have to do . . . when it ought to be done . . . whether you like it or not."* That is the most valuable personal quality.

That personal quality is the true test of character. It distinguishes the "WILLS" from the "WON'TS".

It is a definite requirement for success.

You cannot succeed unless you can make yourself do those three things:

(1) DO the thing you *have to do;*

(2) DO it *when* it *ought* to be done;

(3) DO it *whether you like it or not!*

If you could probe deeply into the personal qualities (or lack of them) among all of *life's failures,* you would find that:

(1) They *failed* because they did not *make* themselves *DO the things they had to do* in order to succeed;

(2) Or they *failed* because they did not *make* themselves DO what they *had* to do—*when it ought to have been done*—in order to succeed;

(3) Or they *failed* because they did not MAKE themselves DO what they *had* to do—*when* it *ought* to have been done—*because they did not feel like doing it!*

Failures usually blame others or conditions (even fate!) for their failures when the almost certain reason for their failures is the clearly obvious fact that *THEY failed to make themselves DO* one, two or all three of the *simple requirements of success* stated at the beginning of this chapter.

Because success is so easy and failure is so tragic, it seems incredible that anyone would *deliberately choose to fail!*

Yet, people *deliberately choose to fail* when they will not even bother to *obtain* and *use* PROVEN SUCCESS METHODS which would *assure their success.* They do not DO what they *have* to do in order to succeed.

And, people *deliberately choose to fail* when they hesitate, delay and wait to *obtain* and *use* PROVEN

SUCCESS METHODS which would enable them to *begin succeeding at once!* They do not DO what they *have* to do —when they *ought* to do it—which is NOW!

Why?

Here's why! For one insufficient excuse or another, *they just don't feel like DOING* . . . what they *have* to do . . . *when* they *ought* to do it!

What should YOU do when *you just don't feel like DOING* . . . what you *have* to do . . . *when* you *ought* to do it?

Do as scientist Thomas Huxley advised: "Acquire the ability to MAKE YOURSELF DO IT."

That is the most valuable personal quality!

Without it you are doomed to failure.

With it you are certain to succeed.

Success is just as simple as *that!*

Chapter 91

Here's HELP! . . .

Selective Psychic Tuning Can Enable You To "Tune In" WHAT YOU WANT!

Everything—past, present and future—exists NOW!

Everything always *has* existed . . . exists now . . . always *will* exist . . . *eternally!*

Nothing is *created!* Nothing *will be created in the future!* Everything *already exists* NOW!

"New" things are not new. They always *have* existed. So "new" things are *discovered—not created.*

Or, things now known to exist are combined or assembled into *"until-now-undiscovered"* combinations. We call these combinations "new" because *we* have just discovered them, *but their unknown presence always has existed, awaiting discovery sometime by somebody.* As part of *Everything.*

This *Everything* which always *has* existed . . . exists *now* . . . always *will* exist . . . is, of course, what is referred to occasionally in this book as *Infinity*.

It is not the purpose of this book to speculate, in depth, on an *Infinity* which limited human intelligence cannot possibly comprehend.

But since each of us is a part of that *Infinity* and since each of us has a channel, through our *subconscious*, to *Infinite Power*—we should, at least, explore the opportunity of *"tuning in"* as much of the Universe as is within the limited *"wave-length"* of human awareness.

The terms *"tuning in"* and *"wave-length"* are used because they are precisely the means *we now use* to tune in the wave-length of some of the things which *now* surround us but of which we are *totally unaware* until we *selectively tune in their wave-length*.

Then we can *clearly see* and *hear* them!

The best known examples are, of course, the sounds of radio, and the pictures and sounds of television.

These sounds and pictures are all around us—originating from the earth, moon and outer-space. *Yet we are totally unaware of any of them until we selectively tune in their wave-lengths*. Only then can we see and hear them although they are there all of the time.

Modern science is rapidly developing the *selective tuning in of many other wave-lengths* in the exploration and discovery of many things in the Universe of which humans have been unaware.

However that is a field outside the purpose of this book and the foregoing example of *selective tuning in* of television and radio *wave-lengths* is adequate for the purposes of this chapter.

The lesson of this chapter is that *everything* NOW exists! *That means that WHATEVER you want NOW exists!*

WHATEVER you want in life is *not* some *"impossible dream."* It NOW *exists!*

You do not have to *"create"* it. You merely have to *"discover"* it because it NOW *exists*—waiting for *you* to *discover* and *possess* it! WHATEVER you want!

The methods by which you accomplish this are clearly explained in the first part of this book (and in full detail in my book: *How To Get Whatever You Want*).

These methods enable you to use your *subconscious* as a channel to *Infinite Power*—*to provide whatever means and opportunities are necessary for you to get WHATEVER you want* if you intensely and constantly *use your subconscious* as taught in this and my other books.

When you use your *subconscious* as your channel to *Infinite Power*, you actually are *tuning in* the *wavelength* of WHATEVER you want.

Remember, WHATEVER you want is *not* some *"impossible dream!"* It already exists NOW—waiting for *you* to *"discover"* it!

You can *"tune in"* the *"wave-lengths"* of WHATEVER you want by using your *subconscious* to turn yourself into a *"human receiver."*

The methods of *selective psychic tuning* through intense, constant *mental pictures,* reinforced by powerful *goal-commands,* are clearly taught in the first part of this book.

I urge you to re-read those chapter lessons.

Your constant USE of them will enable you to GET WHATEVER YOU WANT!

Chapter 92

Here's HELP! . . .

Whatever Your "Calendar Age" Your Body Is Never More Than 100 Days Old!

Now is the time to stop growing "older" by looking at the calendar.

No matter how "old" you are according to your calendar, your body can never be more than 100 days old!

So said no less an authority on aging than Dr. Frederick Swartz, Chairman of the American Medical Association's Committee on Aging.

Specifically, Dr. Swartz stated that medical research has shown that *"no disease entities are due to the passage of time"*.

Then Dr. Swartz said that *no matter what a person's chronological age, most of his body cells are anywhere from a "few days to 100 days old"* at any given time —because cells die and regenerate again and again.

You will learn in the next chapter that "every minute 3 billion brand-new, live, vital cells replace your dead discarded cells—to build a NEW YOU".

Dr. Swartz states that *all* of your body cells are replaced within a 100 days—and that most are replaced much sooner.

So, you start building a NEW YOU minute by minute—and have a completely NEW YOU in 100 days!

The *psychological application* of this astonishing, but medically proven, scientific fact is described in the next chapter and I urge you to study it in the light of the medical opinion of the distinguished Chairman of the American Medical Association's Committee on Aging.

Concerning the infirmities usually associated with aging, Dr. Swartz stated, *"The impact of time (on the human body) is not important,* but the impact of environment is." Your environment is *mental* as well as physical.

He further said that many of the physical and mental infirmities commonly associated with growing old are the result of the absence of good physical and mental exercise programs in the *daily* routines of senior citizens.

The kind and amount of daily physical exercise should have the approval of your physician. My own daily exercises of weight lifting, dynamic tension, isometric contraction, calisthenics and karate practice are a *continuation* of a lifetime of athletics and exercise—and while this demonstrates that reasonably strenuous daily exercise can be *continued* for many years, your doctor's prescription for *moderate daily exercise* will be quite adequate for maintaining physical fitness for a long and healthy life.

You will note that Dr. Swartz also stated that *mental* infirmities commonly associated with growing old are the result of the absence of *daily mental exercise.*

The principal cause of infirmity in the elderly is not the contraction of their arteries but the *contraction of their interests.*

Many old people *discard their interests* as they discard the months on their calendars. So, one after another, their *interests* are tossed into the waste basket of the past. The elderly *contract and limit their interests* to thoughts, places, events and people directly associated with themselves. Increasingly, their interests contract to include only themselves and their ebbing needs and the few people who fill those needs. *Finally, they relinquish all interest.*

It is nature's preparation for death.

However, in the hopeful event that *you* are not preparing to die, but to live—not just exist, but *live*—then you simply *reverse the foregoing process.*

You do not contract and limit your interests— *you maintain and expand your interests* . . . in thoughts, ideas, places, events, activities, and people.

And you do this *beginning NOW . . . whatever your present age.*

It is never too soon or too late to start. The time to start *exercising your mind* is NOW!

In fact, you are making a good start by reading this book. By actually *using* your mind to achieve the MIND POWER objectives of this book, you will *stimulate* your mind . . . you will *discipline* your mind . . . you will *generate terrific mental power* . . . and you will *unleash goal-achieving mental powers* which you did not even know existed!

Add to this the *constant expanding of your interests* in thoughts, ideas, places, events, activities and people—and you will *THINK YOUNG!*

That is the magic Fountain of Youth! . . . THINK YOUNG!

And . . . *LIVE YOUNG!*

If you would *live long,* then *live young!*

You do not have to retire to a rocking chair. You can retire to a new and different career. Or you can retire to extend your established career—but in the manner compatible to your retirement life-style and, best of all, at your own serene, leisurely pace.

Back in the earlier days of our country, when being a millionaire was considered being very wealthy, there was a man named Vanderbilt who owned 12 miles of railroad which was quite a lot of railroad then.

This man, Vanderbilt, was seventy years old, so being past retirement age, he had a lot of time on his hands. He wanted to keep active and interested during his "old age" so he kept busy by increasing the miles of his railroad.

In fact, Vanderbilt, devoted his retirement to increasing his railroad from 12 miles to 10,000 miles and earned a retirement income of more than $100,000,000 which made him richer in his day than practically anybody.

This just goes to show that it pays to do something useful in your "senior years". Your senior years present you with a golden opportunity—and an exciting challenge—to show how "senior" you really are!

There are all kinds of interesting and useful things you can do in your "old age".

Toscanini conducted great symphonies when he was 85.

Edison was still inventing things when he was 84.

Ben Franklin kept interested and busy by helping write the Constitution of the United States when he was 80.

Justice Holmes was still writing Supreme Court decisions when he was 90.

Andrew Mellon was still the nation's leading financier at 82.

Kant wrote some of his greatest philosophical works after he was 70.

Monet was still painting magnificent pictures when he was 86.

Gothe wrote the second part of *Faust* when he was 80.

If none of those senior citizen *occupational therapies* appeals to you, then choose your own *"retirement career"*.

Remember, people do not die because they work too hard. They die because they realize that their lives are ebbing away in a meaningless existence.

The calendar does not determine either your health or the length of your life or your enthusiasm for living it.

Your thoughts do that!
So . . . whatever your age . . .
THINK YOUNG! . . . and LIVE YOUNG!

320

Chapter 93

Here's Help! . . .

Every Minute You Are Changing— For Better Or Worse!

Every minute a part of YOU is gone—*forever!*

Every minute *a part of you dies*—and is discarded. Every minute this dead part of you, in the form of 3 billion worn-out cells, is discarded by your body, nerves and brain. That old, worn-out part of you is gone—*forever.*

And . . . every minute 3 billion brand-new live, vital cells replace your dead, discarded cells—to build a NEW YOU . . . minute by minute!

Obviously, you cannot do this *consciously.*

This building a NEW YOU at the rate of 3 billion new cells a minute is a function of *your subconscious.*

This is why you can change yourself through your subconscious.

Not only does your *subconscious* control the

creating of a NEW YOU at the rate of 3 billion new cells a minute, but your *subconscious* receives 600,000 items—impulse-conveyed bits of *knowledge*—every minute from your nervous system through your brain.

Since your *conscious* mind cannot handle or even be aware of 600,000 items of knowledge a minute, the use and/or memory-storage of this vast inflow of sensorium knowledge also is a function of your *subconscious* mind.

Add to the inflow of 3 billion *physical* cells, the 600,000 items of *sensorium knowledge* EVERY MINUTE and you can have no doubt of the capability of your *subconscious* to create a NEW YOU from these vital new "materials", *the use and control of which is the function of your subconscious!*

That is why this book has constantly emphasized the need for and the methods of directing your subconscious.

Your subconscious is your life-building and your life-control system.

Either you learn and use the methods of directing your subconscious or you are adrift helplessly in a life of confusion and complexity.

It has been the purpose of this book to teach you the PROVEN SUCCESS METHODS of *doing* this—and motivating you to *use* them.

Furthermore, your subconscious mind is a part of the *Infinite Mind,* and is a channel through which you can draw upon the unlimited knowledge and power of *Infinity.* (You may prefer to call *Infinity:* "God", and your use of your subconscious as a *channel* to *Infinite Power:* "prayer".)

Whatever the terminology, the fact is that *your thoughts (mental pictures) create corresponding physical changes.*

This fact has been known, recorded and taught by the GREAT THINKERS throughout the centuries.

It has received its most prolific teachings through the Bible and the sacred scriptures of all of the great religions, some of which have been related in this book.

The fact that each person's life is the product of his thoughts is a cornerstone of philosophy, perhaps best expressed by Spinoza (1632–1677): *"When something happens in the mind, it also happens in the body.* This is called *'psycho-physical parallelism';* that is, mind and body are always parallel, for *they are two aspects of one and the same substance,* which many people call God *which is everything."*

There has been a purpose in listing the preceding facts together in this one chapter.

The purpose is that when we put these facts together, they reveal an answer.

They reveal THE answer!

Let's put the facts together:

(1) Every minute you are changing—for better or worse! *The change is made by your subconscious.*

(2) Every minute 3 billion worn-out cells are replaced in your body by 3 billion new, vital cells. Because your subconscious controls all of your complex bodily functions: your heart-beat, your breathing and all the rest —*the minute-by-minute change in your body cells is made by your subconscious.*

(3) During the same minute that your subcon-

scious is changing 3 billion of your body-cells, your sub-conscious also is receiving from your nerve-system 600,000 items of sensorium knowledge which it uses in guiding your bodily functions and directing your life. *The body changes are made by your subconscious; your life-guidance is controlled by your subconscious.*

Every minute your subconscious is building a NEW YOU and directing your life—which becomes your future.

How can YOU *control* the kind of NEW YOU which your subconscious builds, and its direction of *your* life—which becomes *your* future?

The answer . . .

As taught by all of the *great thinkers* throughout civilization . . . as taught by all of the *great religions* . . . as taught by all of the *great philosophers* . . . as taught by *modern science:* psychological and behavioral . . . *YOU control your subconscious by your constant, intense thought*—which this book defines as *deliberately imagined mental pictures.*

It has been the purpose of this book to teach you the most effective, the most powerful, the most successful methods of controlling your subconscious—because only by controlling your subconscious, can you control your life and your future.

There is no other way!

You must learn and use these methods of directing and controlling your subconscious or you will stumble aimlessly through life, manipulated by others and frustrated by circumstances. The choice is yours. The time is NOW!